What makes this book particularly special to me is its loving, compassionate and optimistic, yet profound outlook on the human condition, our suffering, and our dramas. It puts our everyday struggles into a wider, cosmic, and spiritual perspective. By emphasizing the practical power of forgiveness, gratitude, and other positive qualities, Goran inspires us to trust, love, laugh, enjoy life, and live in peace, despite the perceived obstacles and crises that life throws our way. The book offers hope, love, and optimism. It also shows us how to manage, embrace, and integrate all that we struggle with, and how to connect with and accept our true selves lovingly.

I believe that Goran's teachings can contribute greatly to the healing of individuals and the world. I hope that many people read the book and apply its teachings to their lives—for the sake of themselves, their loved ones, and humanity.

Franziska Mosthaf, PhD

I love the book, and I love reading it. After reading it all the way through for the first time, I immediately started rereading individual chapters that particularly interested me. As a mathematician, I naturally ask myself: Why is that? And the answer lies more on an emotional level than in my rational mind. That's why I use the "honey example" to describe this emotional level to you, dear reader.

You can write or read a doctoral thesis about honey, but the real and profound insight only comes when you dip a spoon into a jar of honey and lick it. Tasting the honey enriches your life with experiential knowledge that is hard to put into words.

It is the same with Goran's book. I read, understand, and *feel* a deep wisdom about life, his life, his being, and his soul. His Integration Technique® enables me to gain insights about myself, my life, my soul, and levels within me that I can't even name yet. It has brought a lightness, joy, and healing to my life on both a physical and emotional level.

A wonderful soul once thanked me after a session for the Integration Technique®, or IT "magic" I used during the session. This magic comes from the technique Goran created and it shines through me in the sessions I give because of its deep transformative power.

Goran, from the bottom of my heart, I thank you for this book, your Integration Technique®, and your being.

Dr. rer. nat. Tobias A. Hartz
Mathematician, ThethaHealing® Instructor (Certificate of Science), Integration Technique® Practitioner (Level 3)

Praise for *Integration Technique® Heal Yourself*

We live in a time of fast changes, with too much information, sudden events that change our daily lives and fast developments in technology and artificial intelligence. Many people feel insecure, confused, and helpless, and existential fear is becoming a common topic in the area of personal and spiritual growth. We see an ever more prominent gap between those who choose a spiritual path and those who live in the victim role, with the idea that they cannot influence their emotions and events in their adventure called life.

Although more than ever is said and written about human behavior, the number of conflicts, manipulation, and misunderstandings between people is rising, with serious consequences for private and business life. Many people feel they urgently need a change, but they are still looking for tools for painless and quick solutions. Working with clients in the area of personal and spiritual growth, I see these topics and challenges. In my individual counseling sessions, every day I encounter dilemmas related to creating life where happiness, peace, contentment, success, harmonious relationships, and abundance on all levels abound. Each of us who deal with growth wants to share with people their experience, learnings, insights and personal truth that will be a signpost on somebody's path towards the life they want to live.

I feel that for many people, this book will become a valuable guide on their path of self-realization, strengthening their intuition and personal power. I believe that Goran's wish that everybody should find love and joy within themselves will reach many hearts around the world through this written word. Changes started knocking at our doors a long time ago; now is the time to feel our light and strength. It is time for people with good intentions and great hearts to connect. Everybody who is holding this book in their hands and is aware of its value is a part of the army of peaceful warriors heading to the fellowship and unity of all people on our planet.

Elvira Mlivić Petrović, PhD
Success and conscious living coach

Integration Technique® Heal Yourself by Goran Karna is like no other book on healing. First of all, it carries a very special vibration. The book itself vibrates with a healing energy. Not only that, the profound love that Goran brings to the world as a healer and teacher also permeates the text.

This is certainly one of the most valuable books on spirituality and healing that I have ever seen. With this book Goran is bringing into our planet a unique and very high healing frequency that is saturated with love. His book is filled to overflowing with life-changing insights, guided experiences and powerful exercises. Yet it does not feel like a dry how-to book. Goran's gentle noble spirit fills the book, making it an uplifting experience of "being with" Goran. It is like you and Goran are hanging out in a coffee shop and having a delightful conversation sprinkled with the golden nuggets of Goran's wisdom.

I highly recommend this book to anyone who is interested in spiritual healing, energy healing, and conventional healing, as well as readers who are on the spiritual path. Even if you are a spiritually awakened person, even if you are a spiritual teacher, you will deeply benefit from this unique and very timely resource.

Today's world needs all the love and healing it can get.

Goran's book delivers!

Ramaji
Spiritual Teacher and Author

In his book *Integration Technique® Heal Yourself*, Goran Karna not only shares his journey from refugee to transformative healer, but he also demonstrates how others can create powerful change in their own lives.

For those looking for practical and accessible ways to start shifting their life from one of struggle and pain to one of freedom, love, and inspiration, let this book be your guide. Goran Karna lovingly shares his heart, wisdom, and decades of spiritual teaching to the benefit of all those seeking to connect with their inner wisdom. The exercises and 'how-to' guidance in this book can be applied immediately and daily. Goran gently invites you to see the truth of who you really are and to love and live from that truth.

Alex Blake, MBA
Founder of Diamond Stories Collection, Engineer, Accredited Transformation Facilitator and Life Coach, Author, Publisher

There are moments in life that silently but profoundly shift the direction of our path. Meeting Goran Karna and being introduced to the Integration Technique® was exactly that moment for me. His Integration Technique® is not just a tool—but a sacred vessel for healing and wholeness. Among all the modalities I've practiced or studied, none has brought me such deep emotional stability and a sense of integration as this one. It speaks not only to the mind or emotions, but directly to the soul—gently realigning all levels of being back into harmony, truth, and peace.

Reading Goran's book is not just an intellectual experience—it's a spiritual initiation. It speaks of things often left unspoken: the depth of grief, the miracle of forgiveness, the mystery of spiritual guidance, the beauty of helping others heal simply by being present. And more than anything, it speaks of humility—that quiet power that is perhaps the rarest of all.

Goran is a guide, a brother, a fellow traveler, a living reminder that healing is not about becoming someone else—it is about remembering who we already are beneath the pain, the beliefs, and the noise.

This book—and the technique it shares—offers something the world desperately needs: a way to return to our essence without bypassing our humanity. A way to live from the soul while staying deeply grounded. A way to serve the world by serving love.

It is an honor for me to walk beside this luminous being in this lifetime. I am deeply grateful for everything Goran has given—to me, to my clients, and to the greater human family. His work continues to ripple through the hearts of many, not through force, but through love. Not through ego, but through service.

Thank you, dear Goran, for showing us that healing is not a destination but a gentle return. For reminding us that our wounds are not our weakness but the gates to our truth. For embodying what it means to be a human being in service of something greater than the self.

May this book find its way into many hands, and more importantly, many hearts. And may your light—steady, clear, and humble—continue to guide us home.

Thank you, thank you, thank you.

Om Tat Sat

Conny Petö Đeneš
Founder of Health Center Harmony, Transpersonal Psychologist, Healer, Artist

I'm thrilled to finally hold Goran Karna's highly anticipated book in my hands. It is essential reading for anyone interested in spiritual growth and healing themselves and the world. In that sense, it is also a necessity. Many people struggle with physical, mental, and emotional issues, fears, insecurity, and a feeling of disconnectedness. The world seems to be increasingly marked by crises: wars, division, climate change, hostility, and a lack of compassion. A broad yet profound view of the world and the individual self, as well as a positive perspective, is surely needed. Goran's insights and wisdom offer a roadmap for personal healing as well as for the development of humanity, peace, and the expansion of consciousness and the universe. The individual and the collective are two aspects that, as Goran convincingly shows, can never be separated.

This book provides many practical, easy-to-follow tools and exercises, primarily from his Integration Technique®, but also from other traditions and modalities. In this sense, the book is also an introduction to the technique, which Goran teaches in depth in his Heal Yourself classes and Integration Technique® workshops.

INTEGRATION TECHNIQUE®

HEAL YOURSELF

ADVICE AND TECHNIQUES TO IMPROVE YOUR DAILY LIFE

GORAN KARNA

INTEGRATION TECHNIQUE®

The information in this book has been compiled as general guidance on the specific subjects addressed. It is not a substitute and not to be relied on for medical, healthcare or pharmaceutical professional advice. Please consult your healthcare professional before changing, stopping or starting any medical treatment. So far as the author is aware the information given is correct and up to date as at June 2025. Practice, laws and regulations all change and the reader should obtain up-to-date professional advice on any such issues. The author and publishers disclaim, as far as the law allows, any liability arising directly or indirectly from the use or misuse of the information contained in this book.

Copyright © 2025 Goran Karna

All rights reserved. No part of this book may be reproduced in any form or by any means, electronic or mechanical, including photocopying, recording, or by any information storage and retrieval system, without permission in writing from the publisher/author.

ISBN 978-0-6454095-7-4

Designed and typeset by David Bradbury (www.dbtype.com.au)
Images courtesy Ave Calvar Martinez (Pexels)

I dedicate this book to my divine teacher,
Sri Sathya Sai Baba

Foreword

As you are certainly aware, we live in very challenging times, some say maybe the most challenging in the recent history of humanity. With global events and pressures of modern life, it is difficult to lead a fulfilled life, remaining in physical and spiritual balance. We need help, and more and more people are realizing that they need to take responsibility for their physical and emotional challenges, and start dealing with them, using adequate tools. We all want to heal ourselves, but few people know how. Goran Karna is a person who knows how, and he is generously sharing his knowledge with us in this book.

The book in your hands is the result and crown of several decades of Goran's life experience, hundreds of seminars, and countless clients he has helped in his healing practice. Whether you are an experienced healer with an established practice, or you are just entering the world of healing for the first time, this book can give you precious tools to improve your life on all levels. It is written in the form of a practical manual that leads you through simple, but very deep and powerful techniques you can use to change your life from the inside out.

The first part of the book introduces you to Goran's life and work, as well as creation of the Integration Technique®. In an honest and simple way Goran tells his life story and its challenges, which have made him the person he is today. The lesson the reader can learn is that even the most difficult life situations can be overcome with faith, self-development, and support of a spiritual teacher. With his personal example, Goran is the best testimonial of the values presented in this book and his Integration Technique® workshops and classes.

Most chapter titles are questions that each person seeking a better life has asked themselves at least once, and most probably many times in their life. If you still haven't found (satisfactory) answers to those questions, this book will provide you with a precious treasure trove of knowledge, insights, and tools. This is not a book you will read in an afternoon and leave to collect dust on your bookshelf. I suggest you read it through and then start trying out the techniques offered in it. They might seem simple at first glance, but their effects are very, very deep. To use them, you don't need any prior experience in healing, just a little time, good will, and an open heart and mind. Once you have tried the exercise of True Acceptance, or the "magic bag" introduced in the book, you will realize your true nature, and have an invaluable tool at your disposal.

Becoming aware of deeply suppressed emotions in your body and transforming them using the Transformation of Consciousness exercise, you will obtain a completely new perspective of your body, realizing that all of those smaller or bigger physical discomforts were just messages you haven't been able to interpret correctly. Once you become aware of that and succeed in it, you are permanently empowered, realizing that the key to healing truly lies within you.

Each following chapter builds upon the one before, and each is ripe with information and insights about topics that concern each human. I hope you will reread them many times and use this information in the best way for you and your life, and persist on the journey of healing yourself.

Silvija Horvat, BA

Contents

	Foreword	xi
1.	**My life**	**1**
1.1	My path and purpose	3
1.2	Why I wrote this book	9
1.3	What motivates me in my life and work	11
1.4	What was my journey into the world of healing like?	12
2.	**Integration Technique®**	**15**
2.1	What is Integration Technique® and how does it work?	17
2.2	How to find solutions to everyday problems	23
2.3	Techniques for visualization, acceptance, and transformation of feelings	26
3.	**Healing and accepting yourself**	**33**
3.1	How healing happens, and the importance of our body in the process	35
3.2	What is the role of parents and their love in healing?	37
3.3	How to accept yourself and free yourself from environmental limitations	39
3.4	How to accept yourself completely	40
3.5	How much do we need support from the universe and others to accept ourselves?	42

3.6	How to heal your heart	45
3.7	How to heal the physical body	46
3.8	How to heal the fetal period	48
3.9	How to heal your inner child	50
3.10	How to heal your soul	53
3.11	How to make contact with your soul	55
3.12	Do we need to heal ourselves first before healing others?	60

4. Living with purpose — 63

4.1	How to live with happiness and purpose	65
4.2	How to move forward with our growth	66
4.3	How to find your deepest inner being	69
4.4	What are the stages of development and who are spiritual teachers?	72
4.5	What is the purpose of people on this planet?	75

5. Love and relationships — 77

5.1	How to forgive your parents	79
5.2	Why do we look for love outside of ourselves?	81
5.3	How to live universal love	83
5.4	How to use truth to solve your problems	85
5.5	How to set healthy boundaries in relationships with others	87
5.6	How to improve your relationships	89
5.7	What is our soul family or family of souls?	92
5.8	How to forgive others	94
5.9	How to find your soul mate or life partner	95
5.10	Who is the right partner for us?	99

6. Spirituality and everyday challenges — 101

6.1	How to reach enlightenment	103
6.2	How to find peace in chaos	106
6.3	How to become free of fear	107

6.4	How to create a better reality and solve financial problems	110
6.5	How to realize your wishes and reach your highest potential	112
6.6	How to rise again after a fall	114
6.7	How to find meaning in life	117
6.8	How to be grateful	118
6.9	How to make the right decision	120
6.10	How to deal with panic attacks	122
6.11	How to find lost motivation	125
6.12	How to find your spiritual teacher and energy technique	127
6.13	How to connect to the present	129
6.14	How to release attachments	131
6.15	How to start the practice of conscious eating	133
6.16	How to live in peace	135

7. Exercises used in this book — 139

8. Integration Technique® Heal Yourself training program — 143

About the author — 149

Where there is faith, there is love;
Where there is love, there is peace;
Where there is peace, there is God;
Where there is God, there is bliss.

– SRI SATHYA SAI BABA

CHAPTER 1

My life

1.1 My path and purpose

When we serve others, we serve ourselves.

It is my wish to introduce you to my life story, so you can perceive me as a real person. I was born in a working-class family in Croatia, in Knin, a small provincial town in the Dalmatian hinterland. My mother worked as a seamstress in a local company, receiving the Best Employee Award, and often helped others who would come to seek her advice. She also supported her own family. Mother was born in a rural area, as one of seven children—she had five sisters and a brother. Her family were small farmers who worked the land, raised cattle, and made traditional leather shoes typical of the area.

My father was also born to a family of small farmers, as the oldest of four sons. His parents had spoiled him, giving him special treatment and importance as the eldest son. He received a business degree from a community college and found a job with the state railway company. He was very sociable, with preference for parties and alcohol. He had his own unresolved issues—feelings of low self-worth—and he was plagued by jealousy and fear of infidelity on behalf of my mother. Although my parents married for love, he was prone to extramarital affairs. From a young age I regularly witnessed fights, arguments, and domestic violence when my father came home drunk. I was born into a problematic family with lots of disagreements and lack of understanding, and I was very fearful as a child. In every photo taken back then, you can see me crying because I felt such lack of love and understanding. I withdrew into my own world and became very introverted, although I loved being with people and having fun.

In elementary school, I tried to take a stand by challenging authority and through rebellious behavior. My grades were excellent, but my behavior was inappropriate. Because I couldn't express myself in my early childhood, in elementary school I was often disobedient to my teachers. They even threatened to expel me.

My sister Natalija was born into our family twelve years after me. I named her, after a girl I liked at that time. Natalija is truly a wonderful person. She was also a wonderful child, and Mother and I did our best to shelter her from daily scenes with our father. I have always loved my sister very much and taken care of her. I am proud that Natalija has become a happy, content person, full of good qualities and virtues. She truly understands the depth of life.

In high school, I quietened down and started thinking about the purpose and meaning of life. When I was sixteen, in a class called History of Civilizations, I heard about Buddhism for the first time in my life. At that moment I felt something touch my heart very deeply. Straight after school I went to the library and borrowed all books on Buddhism written by a Croatian Buddhist and monk in Sri Lanka named Čedomil Veljačić. I read those books, making notes and summaries. Although I belong to the Orthodox Christian church, my parents were Communists, and nobody taught me about God.

In our house we didn't talk about God; there were no religious rituals because both our parents were active members of the Communist Party. My aunt, who lives in Germany now, had me secretly baptized when I was little, because you needed to hide such things in a communist society. Although I had never thought about God before, Buddhism touched me deeply and I realized there was a deeper reality and energy. That is when I realized the existence of being, source, and consciousness, or what different religions call God.

This depth of existence gives meaning to our lives, and it is actually life itself, or life energy. This is the consciousness that is within each and every one of us. After that, I also became interested in Christianity. I started reading about saints and took an interest in Hinduism.

I was turning seventeen and needed to think about choosing my university studies. I had good high-school grades, so I chose to study philosophy and art history in Zadar, a beautiful city on the Adriatic coast. I thought that I would find some answers about existence and life there. In high school I had a great philosophy teacher, named Mane, who taught philosophy with such ease and depth. I thought that philosophy would give me answers to life's questions. I was also interested in art—I visited churches, monasteries and had an interest in old architecture.

However, before university I needed to complete obligatory army service in former Yugoslavia. I was appointed to serve near the town of Tuzla in Bosnia, in anti-aircraft artillery, where I spent one year. It was a very difficult period, during which I became stronger, independent, and learned how to take care of myself.

After my army service, I went to university. I moved into a student dorm and started my four-year university studies. For the first three years I studied and lived in Zadar, and in the last year I commuted from Knin to Zadar weekly because I no longer had the means to live in Zadar.

During my university years, I started studying Indian spirituality. It was then that I discovered a great teacher who became my spiritual and life teacher, the person who inspired me like no other in life. It was Sri Sathya Sai Baba. I read books by Vesna Krmpotić, the greatest Croatian contemporary writer who wrote about India. I embarked on a journey to India for the first time for Sri Sathya Sai Baba's sixty-fifth birthday in 1990, together with 108 people from the area of former Yugoslavia.

I was spending my days at the university in deep thought and contemplation. I was reading works of great philosophers: Plato, Hegel, Heidegger, Aristotle, Kant, and Heraclitus. I spent the nights drinking and talking with my colleagues as we tried to find answers about the meaning of life and life's deepest truths and lessons in our debates. I was fascinated by art and I enjoyed lectures by professors Petrićoli and Vrančić. I was also inspired by Professor Mišćević, who taught modern philosophy and logic. All of them contributed to my experience of a wonderful time at the university.

On top of it all, the university building was situated right at the seafront. I had a great time hanging out with other students. In the very first year I met a girl who was later to become my wife. She was studying to become a primary school teacher. Before that, I'd had no real experience with girls. During my time in the army service, I used to pray at night to meet a woman I could share my life with, both everyday life and spiritually. The two of us remained together for the following twenty-seven years.

My years at the university were the most relaxed and fun period of my life. A tragic event occurred at the end of the third year. My father killed my mother after she asked for a divorce. I received all of that very tragically, as I loved my mother very much. My father was sentenced to eleven years in prison. This changed the course of my life completely. I was a student with no job, my parents had no savings, and suddenly, as a twenty-three-year-old, I was in a position where I had to return to my hometown, look for a job and take care of my eleven-year-old sister.

My mother's murder left me really stricken and with great guilt because I had been persuading her to get a divorce. Through working on myself, I realized it was all about their karmic debt they had to settle between themselves. I had done the best I could in relation to both of my parents. I needed to go through a great process of forgiving them, myself, and God. As a result of that, I started teaching other people about the power of forgiveness.

After that, there was a civil war in the area of former Yugoslavia. It lasted a very long time, and it was a very difficult period of my life. We lived with practically no money. My girlfriend and I were now married and although we were both working, inflation was so high we could hardly buy anything with our salaries. The school where we worked helped us out to get some food on our table. After four years of living in war and poverty, we became refugees and moved to Belgrade, Serbia. We were received there by our acquaintances and followers of Sri Sathya Sai Baba. They provided us with food and board for the first six months until I could find a job. I began working as a sales agent, selling books to companies in Serbia and Bosnia. I would like to use this chance to thank Vojo Stojiljković and his family, who took me into their house, together with my wife and sister.

Later on, I obtained a visa for Australia. I visited my aunt on my mother's side, who lived there, and then stayed on. I completed a course in Yumeiho massage and opened my own business in Australia. I took lessons to improve my English, and then enrolled to study homeopathy at Health Schools Australia. I studied vitamins and minerals and their impact on health, and I received a Diploma in Natural Therapies – Homeopathy.

I visited India in that time to see my teacher. While I was there I studied vibrational healing, which uses cards with homeopathic remedies and vibrations that are inserted into a machine, that then transfers them into pellets that are dissolved under the tongue.

After a few years living in Australia, I met Vianna Stibal, founder of ThetaHealing®, who was teaching a basic ThetaHealing® practitioner's class. The following year I took the advanced practitioner course, as well as the instructor class. Some years later, I received the ThetaHealing® Certificate of Science in America. I learned from the source, from the founder of the technique. I am very grateful to Vianna for those teachings. When I went to the first class, I did not know what kind of a modality it was. My spiritual teacher Sri Sathya Sai Baba had appeared to my wife in a dream and told her I should take that class. The work that Vianna does is of great value for the entire planet.

After that, I returned to Croatia and brought the ThetaHealing® modality to Croatia, Serbia, and Bosnia and Herzegovina. Together with my associates I translated and published all books and manuals for ThetaHealing®. Over 5,000 people took ThetaHealing® classes with me. I gave my contribution to the development of that modality.

While I was still living in Australia, I started practicing different healing modalities. I was looking for ways to help people. It kept me motivated to move forward. I was healing myself through working with clients. I gained a lot of knowledge outside of classes and books and that experience of working with people helped me to develop my own healing modality—the Integration Technique®.

I want to bring this technique to people because it enables them to change their lives in a quick, easy, and simple way. My wish is to help humanity move forward in our evolution. I wish we could be more in touch with ourselves, in contact with our being, our true nature, which is divine, pure, powerful, strong, full of beauty and self-confidence. It is free; it does not manipulate anybody. This technique is a way for humanity to come closer to its being and recognize that being in others. We share the same being; the same soul is within us, the same divine power, and energy. We need to work together, with each other, and not against each other, not only for individual interest. When we accept working for common good, we can have the best lives. Expansion leads us to peace, and we exit the circle of "I" and "mine". The key is to expand toward "we": togetherness where we are all brothers and sisters.

I have shown you my personal growth path, with its many ups and downs. For over thirty years I have been practicing different healing modalities, and I would like to share my insights gathered from that work. This book is a sum of everything—my enthusiasm, my wisdom and my wish to help society, my intuition and personal insights, and gratitude to my teacher Sri Sathya Sai Baba, who gave me particular instructions on how to create this healing technique. He guided me to the path of serving others and showed me a path of light and love in my life. This is the most valuable path, the path of love and service to God and humanity. When we serve others, we serve ourselves. When we serve God in others, we serve God in us. I want to thank my teacher for bestowing me with the honor to share this knowledge with humanity and be the vessel through which this knowledge will come into the world.

1.2 Why I wrote this book

I believe my truth will help someone on their life path.

Why do people do things they love, that fulfill them and make them happy? There is usually no special reason. When you think about it, the reason might be creating something new, or fully expressing everything you carry within, or a wish to contribute to the development of consciousness of humanity. For me, it is my wish to tell my truth through the prism of my life and all the experiences I went through because I believe it will help others.

I've always been opposed to the misconceptions, manipulations, untruths, and prejudice people live by. I never wanted to be a part of that story and, consequently, I lived somehow on the edge of society, never completely accepted, perceived as weird, or at least different from others. I can say that I felt quite flattered by that, which was again one of the traps of my ego—I needed to feel special and different, and if I was not, I would lose my identity. Later on, I realized that each of us is special or unique in our own way, and that true uniqueness is not being different from others—it lies in the way we see the world, ourselves, and others, in acceptance and understanding of ourselves and life, and respect for all creation. Everyone has the right to be special, different, and live in the way they want, but without jeopardizing others.

Maybe the written word is stronger than the spoken word; maybe it can say more, express more, instruct, or provide correct information. We can imagine more; it gives us more time to think, to pause before reacting. I know that the correct information leads to transformation of consciousness and life. On the other hand, incorrect information leads to deterioration of life and consciousness. With the guidance of the highest energies of this universe, in this book I will try to give readers correct information I have gathered in my life through working on myself and others, and through channeling information.

Through this written word I would like to tell everybody that within us we carry happiness and misery, fear, joy, and sadness, and all of it is okay. Through work offered in this book, you will learn how to transform sadness, suffering, and fear into joy, happiness, and love. You will find out how to do that in an easy and efficient way that is available to everybody, with the goal of growth and self-awareness. "Know thyself" is an old Greek maxim I will use here in the sense of getting to know ourselves on all levels of our being—the physical, mental, emotional, and spiritual levels.

Self-suppression, self-ignorance or self-alienation is what happens to most people today. That is why we have crises, why wars happen and now all human stupidity has come to the surface.

Now is the time of change, when we will no longer lose time on an unnecessary life story—the victim story—where we unnecessarily judge ourselves and others, on disputes, inner and outer struggles, conflicts, misunderstandings, resentments, and fears.

The time has come for us to know ourselves, to realize all the power, magnificence, and might of our being, all beauty, dignity, and worthiness. It is time to stand up straight and say we are sons and daughters of God, created in his image, to live in harmony, peace, happiness, abundance, communion, and love.

It is time to preserve this planet and humanity from self-destruction and doom by working together, to tell ourselves and the world we are worthy of living.

This life is beautiful, and we need to share it with others in peace and abundance. It is time to show love in action in our daily life, to direct all our knowledge and wisdom into development and the good of all people. It is time to keep our egos balanced, not letting them rule our lives, not allowing our fears and delusions of the ego to overcome our noble nature, which is full of understanding, knowledge, love and forgiveness. I hope that this work will contribute to the development of all the above, as well as to a better future for humanity.

1.3 What motivates me in my life and work

I do this work because I care that knowledge and light win on this planet and in each individual.

Since my teenage years I have been interested in plant life. I lived in a town surrounded by hills, rivers, and lakes, where lots of wild herbs grew. I used to pick those herbs and dry them to use in winter, and during the war, when we had no green vegetables left, I would harvest edible wild plants. Since an early age, I was attracted to the power of nature and healing. It is difficult to say why—that is something you are born with. It is like some kind of wonder in the world, where you are amazed by all of creation, its innate power and beauty. I don't know if you have ever enjoyed seeing a sick person get well after you shared some words with them, after you have reached out your hand in reconciliation, made them some warm tea or lunch, bought or provided something they needed. I don't know if you know how fulfilling it feels when a person has been living in fear, resentment, guilt, or regret for ten or twenty years, and you help them release that burden in a one hour conversation you had with them. Do you know what it feels like when someone has been sick for a long time, and you helped them feel relief and helped their body be healthy again? Those are the things that fill my soul, heart, and body, and make me feel my life is worth living.

Some people will tell you this is intruding on other people's karma, but I tell you that each healing happens through the energy of creation. Energy heals people from the inside and from the outside, and that is not bad but good karma of being in service to others, to the energy of creation, or the source of everything there is. When the ego intrudes in the healing process and you think you have become the best healer on the planet, then we can talk about bad karma, but egoism, self-importance, and arrogance can cause disturbance in anything we do.

I know that ignorance is the biggest enemy of humanity. Because of ignorance we hate, resent, torture ourselves and others, go to wars, are jealous and envious. They say there is no darkness—only the absence of light. When the light comes in, the darkness disappears.

This light is knowledge. It is a deep understanding of yourself and the light that each of us has within. This is what we came here to learn. Bringing light into my life and the lives of others who want to share the same path with me, is a great motivation for my life and work.

1.4 What was my journey into the world of healing like?

I have been guided and directed.

I have always connected healing with a spiritual path, or spiritual growth. I have never separated those two. Even as a teenager, I spontaneously developed interest in great world religions and books on spirituality. Later on, I practiced different spiritual practices, meditations, chanting God's name, visiting sacred places, meeting holy people, visiting temples, ashrams, and powerful spiritual locations on our planet. Through that I connected with people who were involved in spirituality, and in India I found my spiritual teacher, Sri Sathya Sai Baba.

I used to be a practitioner of Yumeiho, which is a holistic practice of treating the body, and a version of Japanese massage. I studied and practiced homeopathy and natural therapies, and after that practiced ThetaHealing® for many years. Now I have developed my own unique approach to healing, spirituality, and everyday life. It is an approach to living through a wider, different prism than usual.

How did all this happen? I would say that I have been guided and directed. This interest in spirituality and helping people create better lives for themselves is not new; I'd been carrying this within, and it only woke up when I came into contact with different teachings and techniques.

During my recovery from an extended coma in Finland, which doctors induced due to my body's severe reaction to a Staphylococcus infection and coronavirus, I continued to receive ideas and be guided on how to do healing in a different way, a way that combined all my knowledge, teachings, and techniques. As this way was revealed to me,

I took notes, started applying it and started working with people and healing them. That is how I started my healing technique that I now call Integration Technique®. I developed the Heal Yourself training program in four levels and teach this to people all over the world through retreats, workshops, and online webinars.

All of that led me to the path I am now on.

CHAPTER 2

Integration Technique®

2.1 What is Integration Technique® and how does it work?

The technique is based on the philosophy of integrating our individual consciousness, superconsciousness, and subconsciousness with our physical body. It is the alignment and harmonization of body and spirit.

This technique is a result of my thirty years of studying and applying spiritual and healing techniques, psychology, and philosophy, as well as my many years of working with people.

Integration Technique® is both an energy and somatic modality, working with the body. It uses body intelligence to achieve spontaneous healing and raise our consciousness. This technique gets in touch with the suppressed feelings we, as humans, carry in our bodies without being aware of them. This technique transforms them and releases the energy. By working with the body, the technique also balances male and female energies within us, it develops and stimulates female energy within us, which is gentle, playful and powerful at the same time.

The four pillars of the Integration Technique®

1. BODY WISDOM

Our body is intelligent and carries in its cells all memories, feelings, and traumas we have ever lived through. It also has all the knowledge necessary to heal our emotional, mental, physical, and spiritual life. Through working with the body, we get in touch with the deepest parts of our being, and we develop self-confidence and self-respect.

The key to everything lies within our body. All the answers, truths and insights necessary to move forward are inside of our body.

2. ACCEPTANCE

When we truly accept our emotions and challenging situations in our life, then those emotions and situations transform into higher energies and vibrations. True acceptance happens when, instead of rejecting and fighting the past, people, or emotions, we embrace and welcome them in our life and become grateful for their existence. This is what instantly liberates us.

By accepting ourselves as we are, we can overcome and transform life's obstacles and create space for healing, growth, and a happier and balanced life to naturally happen.

3. HEALING

In this modality, healing can be emotional, physical, mental, and spiritual, and it happens quickly and spontaneously. Deep, hidden, and suppressed feelings are transformed using body awareness into positive emotions and virtues that have a positive impact on our health. Therefore, we become more balanced and harmonized, more grounded, stable, creative, and positive about our life.

Healing happens when we realize there is actually nothing

wrong with us—that our true nature is accepting, loving, and in harmony with everything within and around us.

4. GROWTH

This method of healing uses our life's circumstances, disappointments, stress, loss, trauma, and financial or relationship difficulties for our inner growth or for raising our vibration. We believe that every situation in our life is very important, and it brings us an important message. When we realize it and accept it, then a real shift in our consciousness happens. The reality in which we live, changes from fear and resentment to love, creativity, joy, playfulness, and ease of existence. We can manifest and perform better in everyday life.

Our experiences, thoughts, and feelings lead us toward our growth, not away from it.

The technique encompasses the integration and healing of all five inner bodies, known as koshas: physical body, energy body, mental body, wisdom, and bliss body. This leads to expansion of consciousness and realization of our being. The basic working principle is acceptance and transformation of feelings, thoughts, habits, inclinations, traumas, and different patterns of behavior and action, everything we think is undesirable in ourselves, everything that has happened in our lives and is happening now. Instead of rejecting all of that, denying or suppressing it, it is all transformed into higher consciousness and qualities we already have within, and we become aware of them. Everything should be accepted and welcomed with intimacy. We use visualization exercises, as well as our abilities of comprehension and intuition. We use intelligence of our physical body, inner bodies, and highest consciousness to facilitate self-healing and natural growth and development of consciousness.

This technique offers a simple way of resolving emotional blockages (such as fears, remorse, regret, guilt, dissatisfaction, bitterness) and disorders like depression, anxiety, and similar states. All of those feelings and disorders are here because they have a message for us, something important that we need to realize, to understand. The reason why we do not accept ourselves and the world, why we judge ourselves and others is just ignorance, or not seeing the bigger picture, not understanding what is really happening.

When you offer somebody a different perspective on what is happening in their life, the person can then change their perspective and let go of suffering. We let go of suffering when we realize that we have other options in life, that other choices are possible, when we completely accept ourselves, our life, and others, and realize that we do not lack anything. To suffer means to be separated from love, from God. Everything we would like to achieve in our lives emotionally and spiritually is already integrated in our cells—we just need to remember it. Of course, we are always led and helped throughout the process by the energy of creation, or God, or highest consciousness.

Healing and manifestations of anything in our lives are swift and efficient. We will learn how to use our manifestations to contribute to our growth, how to manifest from the soul—how to realize the wishes of our souls. It is a quick way of growth and development, which does not require any special discipline or giving up on life's pleasures.

This technique helps us realize our full potential, connect with our soul, our higher self, the divine part of ourselves, and live the highest truth of ourselves.

It helps us accept or realize the qualities of our soul or the divine part in our daily life, so we can live our highest purpose and meaning. In other words, our complete spiritual knowledge is integrated into our life, so we can live it with joy and love, and become the best versions of ourselves, living in the unity of thoughts, feelings, words, and deeds, with our hearts, minds, souls, and ego walking the same path of growth and love. We can live in a high vibration of consciousness, light, and peace.

Consciousness is something common to all beings. Everybody is conscious. The same energy of life or consciousness permeates all. What is different is the outside form, thoughts, names, and the roles we play. Just like the wave is a part of the ocean, we are a part of divine consciousness. We look different for a moment, then we go back to where we originated, and emerge again as a wave, but we have never been separated from the ocean, or God, or consciousness. All creation comes from consciousness: the entire universe, time and space are just manifestations or expressions of the highest consciousness. Consciousness is in the background of our thoughts, words, deeds, and feelings as energy, which is the basis, or witness, of everything. It is the observer, but at the same time a participant in everything that is happening. Consciousness wants to express itself through us, to manifest fully; it wants to remember itself. This is the energy of universal love, that all life is based upon. This is the being of the universe. All life is evolution, development, or return to the self, to one's true nature, in perceiving and living the unity of existence. All creation is a manifestation of consciousness, which has always been there and always will be. This consciousness in each of us individually is our being, and through this technique we go into our being or consciousness and let it express itself, manifest itself through us and heal us completely.

According to ancient Vedic writing, each of us has inner energy layers or sheaths, known as koshas, which go from the periphery of our physical bodies to the center of the self or consciousness. Each layer represents one aspect of our being, and each one is very important for our life, health, and spiritual growth. All of these layers are conscious: they have their own intelligence, feelings, knowledge, and understanding. All of them are interconnected and influence the development of consciousness. To develop our being fully and realize our full potential, we need to heal, harmonize, and integrate all those bodies, let go of our identifications with them and let the highest consciousness within us fully express itself through us.

The first kosha is made of the food we consume and represents the physical body. As we start becoming aware of our bodies, we feel we are present in the body, and we become more centered and grounded, less prone to dissatisfaction and more conscious of which food and activities are good for our bodies. We become present in the now.

The second kosha is the so-called energy body. When we are relaxed or observe our breath, we can feel waves of energy flowing through our body. We can perceive that our body is larger than the boundaries of our skin, and we can perceive contact with the vital energy, prana, or chi. This energy moves through the body through a network of energy channels. It controls the movement of blood, body fluids, digestion, respiratory system, and heart function. It gives us vitality and we can more easily connect with the energy in nature and energies of other people. Feelings of being energized and calm are the qualities of this energy body.

The third kosha or mental body is made of thoughts, images, perceptions, and emotions in your inner world. Deeper levels contain powerful mental structures that form beliefs, opinions we have absorbed and accumulated from our families and group consciousness of the society we live in. They represent mental patterns that shape our lives.

The fourth kosha, the wisdom body, is made up of intuition and consciousness. It lets us move away from the current situation and look at it from a broader perspective and feeling of inner knowing, which comes from this body. It is responsible for deep intuitive insights and realizations. When you create something, express yourself creatively, when you write, paint, solve problems and life situations, you come into contact with this body. It is here that we stop identifying ourselves with thoughts and feelings and become a witness of the mind and our lives.

The next layer after the true self or consciousness is the fifth kosha, the bliss body. It is the consciousness of existing as a complete and integrated being, just as we are. Happiness and joy are natural states of being. This is the last layer that stands between the individual consciousness and universal oneness. This state of bliss or deep peace can be experienced in states of deep meditation or complete immersion in what we are doing, when we lose sense of time. When you are in contact with the bliss body you are joyful, free, and content. When you are in the bliss body, you realize through your experience that love is the deepest reality.

2.2 How to find solutions to everyday problems

> *Our happiness and peace have never been in the hands of others—society, media, our parents, or partners.*

We wonder how to grow when the situation in our environment is chaotic, when there are uprisings, war, and fears. We wonder how to solve everyday problems in our lives, how to overcome fears of group consciousness, subconscious programming that says we must suffer because Jesus suffered, that suffering and poverty bring us closer to God, that we develop through conflict and drama. We ask ourselves how to stop running and burying our heads in the sand, how to keep balance and calm when everything around us is the exact opposite of that. We wonder how to be authentic, not succumb to the influence of media, keep our sanity, and not run away from reality into books, spiritual teachings, and solitude.

When we turn on the radio, we tune into the frequency that suits us best, that feels best to us. Similarly, there are different frequencies surrounding us: frequencies of love, peace, Divine presence, or, as it is trendy to say, the frequency of the present moment. However, there are also frequencies of fear, worry, dissatisfaction, and grief.

How we tune our radio receiver depends on us, on our preferences, likes and dislikes. Similarly, what goes on inside of our heads also depends on us, because we have the freedom of choice—to choose the frequency of peace or fear, love or agony, joy or sadness. Our focus or choice of the radio station is in our own hands. Not others.

Our peace depends solely on tuning into the right frequency, on our focus on what is positive and good, on our realization that we have freedom of choice and are not forced to suffer and be unhappy.

Reality of love and Divine presence is like a sweet and tender cake that is offered to everybody to try, to taste it and experience it. Let's tune into that frequency and let other frequencies be what they are; they also have their purpose and importance. I am not offering you something that is up in the clouds; divine reality is real, just like your worries and fears are real. Worries and fears come and go, but

Divine presence is always there—it doesn't go away. It has always been here and always will be. It does not change; it is full of exhilaration, beautiful, eternal, and loving. When our lives are full of disappointments because of unfulfilled expectations from the self and others, when suffering is weighing us down, when worries overwhelm us, when we have so many losses in our lives and our bodies have become sick, it is difficult to talk about Divine presence as a way out of our life situation. For many people it is as far-fetched as the stars in heaven. That is completely natural and human. That's why we will go step by step to resolve our life dramas.

Let's say that the cells in our bodies remember all our experiences from our birth onwards, and even before birth, from the fetal period. Our cells or our DNA store all our memories of our higher consciousness, our soul, our divine consciousness, or, simply put, all the love, contentment, happiness, peace, and joy of existence are already in there. A veil was created over our eyes because of all that has happened to us, our focus on those events, and because nobody has told us that the treasure we seek is not in the outside world, but within us.

We don't have the complete picture of our lives and what is happening in them. That is why we have such experiences instead of some others. That is why we have the feeling we have missed some chances, and some things should not have happened. We feel we have been wronged, and the universe is against us. It is important to change that story and see the real state of affairs.

Everything that has happened and is happening right now has a message for us, and it will keep happening until we hear the message and accept it into our lives. Everything that has happened remains recorded in our subconsciousness, and our cells and our DNA carry those memories. It is important to ask your body to tell you the message or meaning of your experiences and feelings that were created there.

It is important to become aware of that meaning in your body, and in that way discover why something has really happened, or realize that it all made sense and worked for us. The true answer is always growth, development, and expansion of consciousness. When you embrace that as true, as a part of your being and life, it is different than when you hear it from others.

The key to everything lies within our body. All the answers are there; all the truths, all insights necessary to move forward are inside of our body—not in books, theories, and techniques. Everything we want to resolve regarding our emotional, mental, or physical health is in there. There is even the solution that leads us to abundance of everything in life, to complete happiness, financial growth, spiritual realizations of all kinds, healing of relationships and traumas. There are manifestations, creations, all the love and beauty of this world.

The universe has given us bodies, and through the body, it has made us worthy of it. There is plenty of everything; nothing is lacking in us, in our body and our being. When I say "our body", I also mean our higher self, or our higher consciousness, and our soul, our conscious and subconscious mind, divine consciousness, or life energy, as well as all of our energy bodies. I also include that which we call our personalities, or "I". None of that is separated from the body, from our cells or our DNA.

To work with the body and resolve our daily problems, I was given several simple visualization exercises you can use as first aid in all life situations you wish to resolve or improve. These techniques are simple, without any mysticism, and anybody can learn to do them. My wish is to offer the world a simple way of self-development to improve your life and become aware of your true nature.

The exercises below can be used for any emotional problem, trauma, fear, relationship problem, financial problem, health problem, and for manifesting. They help us discover blockages in our physical bodies and inner bodies (energy body, mental body, wisdom body and bliss body), and transform those blockages into qualities, light, and power of our own being. There is harmonization and healing of all those bodies, which serves the process of realization of our soul. The process is simple, and anyone can learn and master it.

The goal is to discover for yourself the greatness of your own being through acceptance, understanding, transformation and integration of everything we carry within. The purpose is to integrate in our everyday life everything we have learned or become aware of as already existing within us. The goal is also to become aware of where the problem comes from—which events in our life, which feelings, and are those feelings our own or taken over from our mother, father, group consciousness, nation, or ancestors. When we bring the light of awareness to a problem and see the higher perspective of what has happened, the problem loses its gravity and significance for our lives.

2.3 Techniques for visualization, acceptance, and transformation of feelings

The goal is to integrate all we have learned and become aware of into our daily lives.

These exercises are designed to help you resolve and transform everyday issues and feelings.

✥ Exercise. True Acceptance 1

The purpose of this exercise is acceptance of life problems, unresolved issues from the past and present, emotional concerns, relationship problems, things we have been trying to achieve for years without success, things we believe we lack, feelings such as guilt, fear, regret, remorse, and rejection.

Imagine putting all of those unresolved issues in a bag, then hugging the bag like you would hug a loved one. Then say to that bag: "You are a part of me; you are mine. I accept you; I do not reject you. You have an important place in my life. You are divine. God loves you. Mother and father love you. I am grateful for your existence. Stay with me as long as you like. You came to me with a divine purpose. I love you."

We repeat this until we feel intimacy with the contents of the bag and the bag is completely emptied. In this way, instead of fighting the unresolved issues in our life, we accept them and transform them, and they no longer represent a problem when we look at them.

❧ Exercise. True Acceptance 2

This exercise is about accepting all the good qualities we have inside of us, but we may not be aware of them all, or we haven't truly embraced them into our lives. Put in your bag love, peace, pleasure, gratitude, courage, kindness. Then hug the bag like you would hug a loved one, saying: "You are a part of me; you are mine. I accept you; I do not reject you. You have an important place in my life. You are divine. God loves you. Mother and father love you. I am grateful for your existence. Stay with me as long as you like. You came to me with a divine purpose. I love you."

Feel those qualities becoming a part of yourself, part of your being, part of your identity, and feel them filling each part of your body, entering all your cells, blood, soul, heart, DNA, everything you are, all of your bodies.

❧ Exercise. Transformation of Consciousness

Find a place in your body where you feel the negative emotions that trouble you. Then see how those emotions look—do they have a shape or color? What is their shape and color? What is their texture—soft or hard? Is this a living energy or not?

When you have made certain this is a being or living energy, ask this energy what it wants to tell you, what kind of message it is bringing into your life. When you find out or receive the message, if the message is negative, keep asking until you come to a positive message. Then ask yourself how you feel when you hear this message. For example, your emotions want to tell you they are protecting you. Ask yourself: "How do I feel when I am protected?" The answer might be something like: "I feel safe, proud, strong and peaceful."

Become aware of those feelings in your body. Locate them in a certain body part and when you have become aware of them, let those feelings flow through the whole body. If you encounter fears, negative thoughts, and feelings, just let them be there, and go deeper beyond them until you become aware of the positive feelings.

If you cannot feel them in the whole body, ask the energy of creation or your being to show you those feelings in the whole body, in every cell, every organ, in your blood and DNA. When this happens, you should observe the emotions that used to trouble you from this position of new feelings, and feel they no longer trouble you. There is a transformation of feelings and consciousness.

If you cannot feel a certain quality or virtue within yourself, ask to have that feeling inside you increased by

100 per cent, or as much as is optimal for you in that moment. Ask to be shown the blockages that prevent you from becoming aware of those feelings and qualities. Then work on those blockages.

❧ Exercise. Entering Your Heart or Being

Bring your consciousness to the area of your heart; feel the energy of love or light. Visualize your being as a big sea or ocean within your heart. Imagine yourself on the surface of this ocean. Then go deep down into the sea, into your being, and slowly sink, delve into the depths where there is absolute peace, or consciousness, or light. Come down to the bottom and rest there; rest in yourself. Feel deep peace, eternal existence, the endlessness of your being.

Now take a look at your fears, anger, dissatisfaction, and traumas from this position, from where you are now. You can visualize all those feelings on your body or in front of your body or put them in a bag. You can also say, "I am looking at the courage and love inside of myself," while you are at the bottom of the sea or ask, "May I have this virtue, feeling… shown to me in my body?" Notice what you feel in each cell of your body.

❧ Exercise. Intuitive Insight

We can ask to be shown anything that we cannot see, feel, or become aware of, whether it is a feeling, event, quality, or virtue. We can also ask for the highest truth—to be shown the highest truth about something that is unclear, such as why something happened, or what really happened.

In that way we gain a broader perspective, insight, or vision of something, and we release limitations of any kind—emotional, mental, and spiritual. We can give an intuitive insight to another person when we give them a different, broader picture of what is bothering them, tell them something from a different angle, with good intentions of helping them. Sometimes when we say just one word with the intention of encouraging the person to think about something, this can change their life.

❧ Exercise. Direct Method

When we have a problem in our life, (for example we can't forgive someone, we don't have enough money to live, or we are sick) we ask how we would feel if the situation were the opposite (if we forgave someone completely, had plenty of money, or were healthy). Become aware of those feelings, then locate them in a certain body part and become aware of them again.

If we cannot become aware of them because of other negative feelings, we let the negative feelings remain where they are and ask to be shown what is behind or under them until we become aware of the initial positive feelings, first in this body part, then in all cells of the body. Stay with those feelings until they completely permeate your entire being. Then look at your previous problem from this position.

Exercise. Gratitude and Grounding After Your Self-Session

Say to yourself: "My heart is filled with love; I am grounded and belong fully to my body. I am truly grateful to myself, to consciousness, energy of creation, laws, and God's grace for this healing. Thank you all. I feel comfortable and at ease with all of these changes. I recognize, accept, and keep this healing. I am worthy and deserving of God's love and of this healing. I have the support of my ancestors, of the laws, and my soul family for this healing. I am asking the grace of the universe to integrate the healing in each of my cells, in everything I am and in all of my bodies. I am grounding."

Imagine roots growing into the earth from your feet and your entire body, from the base of your spine.

Say "thank you" once again at the end.

You can use all these exercises in your daily life, for your healing, and I will mention them again in this book.

CHAPTER 3

Healing and accepting yourself

3.1 How healing happens, and the importance of our body in the process

It is natural to feel healthy, to feel good in your own skin, to feel happy, content, joyful, fulfilled, and at peace with yourself and the world.

Healing happens when people are ready to accept it, when they really want it, when they are open and ready to let the energy of creation or life energy heal them. Energy of creation heals us from the inside and from the outside, and when the two combine, there is spontaneous healing, which is a natural thing. It is natural to feel healthy, fulfilled, and at peace with yourself and the world. Everything that's the opposite of that is unnatural. We should let our nature come to light and allow this force of creation to do what it does—everything that is necessary so we can have physical, emotional, and spiritual health.

Healing is a natural phenomenon. When I work with people, I help them to allow themselves to heal, to accept it, and that is all. It is about a change in perception, a change of neural pathways, opening to new insights, perspectives, new understanding, opening to new, fresh energies to come into our space, into our world.

I've taught this technique to thousands of people and watched them heal their broken bones, respiratory and urinary infections, reproductive and nervous systems and relationships. To give you some examples, a male client had a problem with his ankle that had been going on for thirty years. After doing a healing session with me his ankle was returned to a completely healthy state. I have another example of a lady who was struggling with her relationship with her mother, and after two sessions with me her relationship was markedly improved. Another lady came to me seeking help to sell her land after trying to sell it for ten years without success. After completing my level 2 class she sold the land easily and immediately. These are just a few examples of the power of this technique.

Emotional, mental, and physical healing happens simply and spontaneously. People are usually fascinated by physical healings. I have had many such experiences, but healing is also the disappearance of fear, hatred, resentment, the feeling of being used, the feeling of being unloved that you have carried your whole life. When you change that and let yourself feel happy and loved, that is a great healing. It is a huge thing that happens to people once in a lifetime, and some people never experience it. Healing of physical problems, such as a broken bone, pneumonia, inflammation in the liver, kidney, or any other organ, is the same as healing mental or emotional issues.

The most important thing is human faith that it is possible; this faith enables the healing to happen.

When people are ready, healing comes quickly and easily.

Sometimes healing does not happen because the illness is serving the person, that is, they subconsciously want to remain sick, although they visit one healer after another, investing a lot of money, energy, effort, and time into their healing. Deep down in the subconscious, it serves the person not to be healed. For some people, it is a way to receive attention, love and care from others, which they did not have before, so they attract those energies. Many people grow through illness; they start taking better care of themselves, ponder the deeper meaning of life, think about themselves and their life, about the changes they might make. All those experiences serve people to grow and move forward, so they remain sick. This can be changed by understanding that they can also achieve that growth when they are healthy, not only when they are sick.

I have realized one thing: we carry so many suppressed feelings that block our healing, and we are unaware of them. We carry those feelings in our bodies, and this is why I have focused my work on becoming aware of those feelings and their transformation. Our bodies are intelligent, and they carry in their cells all memories, feelings, and traumas we have ever lived. They have all the knowledge necessary for healing our emotional, mental, physical, and spiritual life. We use body intelligence to facilitate spontaneous healing and raising consciousness. Through body work we come into contact with the deepest parts of ourselves, or our being, and develop feelings of self-confidence and self-respect. In addition to that, through body work we balance male and female energies within us, we develop and foster female energy, which is gentle, playful, and powerful at the same time.

I have realized that in our physical and inner bodies we have all the qualities we need for life, and those qualities create our reality once we recognize them within ourselves. So, our bodies are like portals and tools for healing and the realization of our being.

3.2 What is the role of parents and their love in healing?

Our relationship with our parents influences our relationships with ourselves and others.

The love of our parents is a fundamental issue of life, and this topic deeply influences human life. It is emphasized when we feel that we were not loved as children, that love was not equally distributed among children, or nobody received it because parents were self-absorbed and neglected us. This is the feeling that we were abandoned, neglected, lonely, unloved, and unwanted since childhood. It permeates our entire lives very deeply.

In my opinion, healing this relationship is the most important part of a person's complete healing. This relationship influences our relationships with others, partnerships, relationship with ourselves, our professional success, success in the world, and in all areas of life. On a deeper level, we need to understand that we were loved and accepted by our mother and father in the best way they knew how to. Once we accept that, new possibilities and new areas of life will open up to us, new energies will enter our lives, our finances, and our emotional and physical health will improve.

This is a new driving force, because our mother and father are like the mother and father of the universe, like earth and the sky, Divine Mother and Father, like the two principles—male and female—the entire universe is based on. If we do not receive that energy and allow it to flow naturally, there is stagnation in everything. In that case, everything is going to be much more difficult than it should naturally be.

The significance of our relationship with parents is connected to the feeling of worthiness, and it marks all areas of our lives. This relationship influences our health, finances, and success in business and partnerships. It is the same as our relationship with planet Earth. The Earth gives itself selflessly, because without Earth, there is no life. In the same way, your mother gives you life, and that influences all areas of your life. A part of the healing of that relationship is the healing of the heart. If we don't resolve the feelings we carry in our emotional heart, our physical heart will suffer.

❧ Exercise. Feelings of Worthiness

> Relax and take a deep breath in. Focus on the area of your heart, solar plexus, or forehead. Tell the highest consciousness that you request to be shown what your mother and father felt in the moment of your birth. Imagine that you are entering their physical and emotional hearts. Ask to be shown what they were feeling. First go to your mother, feel her thoughts, and ask to be taken into her heart, to feel that deep love every mother has for her child. Notice how you feel in your

own heart. You will feel the warmth of your mother's love healing your heart. Do the same with your father, asking the highest consciousness or life energy to show you what your father felt in his heart when you were born.

If you have never met your biological father or mother, know that it has no influence on this exercise. Everybody has a mother and a father; even if you have never known them, go into their hearts. It is okay if you feel their worries and fears; go deeper. When you feel love, focus on your heart and on your mother's and father's love. Feel it healing your heart. This will give you an immense feeling of worthiness, and with that feeling, you can achieve anything in life. Now is the chance to accept the feelings of love and being loved.

3.3 How to accept yourself and free yourself from environmental limitations

Individuals that have contributed the most in the history of humankind have stood out and been different.

Each person should make important decisions for themselves and not let their environment smother their life, inner aspirations, and wishes of how to live their life. The key is to live from inside, to live your own life. We have the ability to resist; each of us could say no to what is against our beliefs, but because of fear, many people do not stand up for themselves. People are afraid of not being accepted, of rejection or losing their job.

It is important to know that you can act irrespective of fear. Fear can be overcome when you work on yourself, because every fear is unrealistic and very limiting. When a person is acting from fear, they receive and realize much less than they would if they acted irrespective of the fear. A simple way to overcome fear is to understand what it is we are afraid of, find out where the fear is coming from, become aware if we have accepted other people's fears. Those fears most often come from our parents, society or something that happened to us in childhood or in our mother's womb. When fear comes from several different sources, it can go very deep, even to the soul.

Despite fears, a person can act in the direction they believe is right. It can always help us when we believe that what we are doing and what we want is right, that it is right to stand up for yourself, make your wishes and dreams come true, that it is right to express yourself and how you feel. This is more important than what somebody will say, how society will react if we are different, whether they will label or reject us.

What people really want is freedom from fear, limitations, and any kind of coercion. To realize all of that, it is necessary to accept yourself, know what you want and move in that direction. People who love us will stay, and those who don't accept us will go away and keep rejecting us. This is the solution for how to resist the influence of society.

You should not resist but be authentic instead.

3.4 How to accept yourself completely

The most important thing is to understand yourself.

I have seen and witnessed how people who work on themselves and want to grow often divide themselves into good and bad beings. They judge themselves for something they did or did not do, and they also judge other people, which results in many relationship issues.

The key is to start accepting yourself, which means to be at peace with all parts of your personality that need to be understood, and not judged. Understanding is the basis for acceptance. True and deep acceptance of yourself and others does not mean unthinkingly following something somebody told you. The most important thing is to understand yourself, to know that what you feel and who you are is okay, that it is a part of your whole, of complete physical, mental, emotional, and spiritual being. When we see ourselves as a whole, everything that occurs on those levels is completely okay. Nothing is sinful, or against God and the world. Nothing that we are can be against our existence, because it is a part of our life. In that sense, it is important to understand that we judge ourselves not because we felt, did or thought something wrong, but because other people judged us and we accepted questionable societal norms.

Social norms, norms of group consciousness, and even religious norms are very questionable. Although unquestioning acceptance of norms is harmful, it does not mean that we should be irresponsible and do harmful things. It is important to accept ourselves without questioning, because who and what we have has been sent from the universe. Whether you believe in God, energy, or life itself, existence is there.

We should understand and accept that which is bothering us and transform it into something positive. Fighting it, accusing yourself, blaming yourself, and accepting judgment means stagnation and struggle. Not accepting yourself is pure suffering. One of the main reasons for suffering is when we do not accept what is happening in our lives. People often think that if they accept their anger, rage, and fear, they will not move forward in their growth. It is okay to be in fear; it is okay to be angry. It is okay and human for any kind of feelings to occur.

It is also human to make mistakes; it is not like perfection is the only thing that's good enough. It is human to do something stupid, but it is much more natural to forgive yourself and others, to understand and accept yourself, and therefore others, than to judge. This part of us that we perceive as bad is actually some kind of purification that is happening in the deeper levels of our being and helps us move on. If we accept that and understand it in this way, we have the possibility to move forward. If we understate or judge those things we don't like about ourselves, we suppress them so we can be righteous and good. In that way we create inner strife and conflict that lead us to disease and hinder our growth.

Another aspect people don't understand and are unaware of is that we do not accept the beauty, depth, and grace of our being. Nobody has told us that we have within us enormous abundance, depth, greatness, and value that is timeless, regardless of how much money we have made, how much success we have achieved, how much recognition in the world and acceptance from others we have received, how happy we are in our family life and other relationships. They haven't told us or brought our attention to the fact that we are eternal, indestructible beings who came to this planet to help ourselves and others grow and prosper, to celebrate life, to rejoice, to enjoy each other and life. People are not aware of those deep values and beauty they carry within. We need to accept and discover that; it is something we all have, and yet we live in ignorance and illusion, under a veil that has covered us because we have invested all our attention and energy into some other things in life.

To accept yourself, it is important to write down everything you dislike in yourself, that you think is not okay, or is not a positive aspect of your being. Then decide to accept that. Simply tell that part of your being that you accept it, love it, that it is yours and it should stay with you as long as it wants. Accepting yourself means you love that part of yourself, that you are intimate with all your flaws, negativities, fears, feelings, habits, and thoughts. Tell each part of yourself that you love it, like you would tell your favorite person on this planet. Accept everything that bothers you, that causes regret, remorse, guilt, feelings of lack, feeling that something is wrong with you, or that you are not worthy of good things and a good life. This inner conflict creates many feelings that overwhelm us and all our thoughts and focus go in this pointless direction, in a vicious circle, instead of using our energy for productivity, creativity, progress, development, and moving forward with life.

3.5 How much do we need support from the universe and others to accept ourselves?

It is important to be what we are, to be in harmony with ourselves, our inner being.

The universe supports things that are honest and true, or better said, the universe supports everything that is natural, relaxed, in touch with itself. If we look at nature, we see how the trees, birds, and animals are taken care of. They are provided for; they live naturally, and everything unfolds as it should. Not living your true nature, not living freely, not feeling free, not being what you are, not expressing yourself, not letting yourself express fully—all of these things are unnatural. They are unnatural and thus not supported by the universe. The truth is exactly the opposite. It is important to be what we are, authentic, in touch with our inner being, our wishes, thoughts, ambitions, and we don't need to change ourselves to be accepted. It is important to accept what you are and live in harmony with the universe, to be honest with yourself, live in truth and harmony with nature and the entire universe, not just a small number of people and limited group we find important. In the beginning, people may not like you being authentic and they will show disapproval, but later on they will realize that you have achieved what they could not, and they will give you credit for achieving things they did not give themselves permission to achieve.

People often don't allow themselves to be who they are because they are limited and blocked from all sides, and they don't know how to deal with that. Our task is just to take the first step, because that leads us into deep healing and propels us forward. There is a huge shift in consciousness because we can then be what we are, and we don't worry about what others will say any longer. We are aware that they are just their reactions and that we are not responsible for others, but for our lives only. We have to get our lives in order, in harmony with all existence. It is much easier to live your own life than live the lives of other people, your parents, or your environment. In the long term, their lives cannot bring you happiness or fulfillment. If we adjust because of the environment we live in, we dampen our true nature. This is of no use to anyone and does not help our growth.

By accepting ourselves, we gain a sense of freedom from limitations, from being slaves to fears, to prejudices we were taught by others, and we agreed to believe in. We gain freedom from seeing ourselves as bad, as wrong, from thinking there is something wrong with us, and we become aware of our beauty and goodness. The realization that everything around us is just as it should be makes us free. In this way, we are freed from a huge burden. Joy and the realization that we are good, just as we should be, awaken within us.

We often carry resentment toward ourselves, and guilt, regret, and remorse. We think that we could have done something differently. Freedom from such thinking is the freedom everybody is talking about in the spiritual world. All great spiritual teachers have spoken about this freedom. Few people understood Jesus when he spoke about freedom, so they wanted freedom from the outside—they wanted to free the Jews from the Romans—but I believe he was talking about the inner freedom, where you feel unity with the entire universe. This is where you feel you are okay, that you are all sons and daughters of God, that your life is beautiful, and not something bad, sinful, limited, unhappy, dark, muddy, or impure. This is complete freedom of spirit, freedom of consciousness, freedom of life. This kind of freedom is the awareness of the huge expanse of our being, huge strength and greatness that has been waiting to break free and manifest in our everyday life. We should accept this freedom as a part of our lives and then act from this position, instead of acting from fear and feelings of dissatisfaction, lack, and emptiness.

Accepting yourself completely means valuing your strength, knowing yourself, feeling how strong you are as a being, just as everybody around you is as well. This means respecting yourself as a powerful being, as well as everybody else, because all life is the creation of the Divine. This is deep respect of life, deep respect of yourself, of God, of the entire creation. It is the ultimate giving of yourself, because everything deserves our attention, even the smallest thing. Each detail of our life becomes important. Everything we do should fulfill us, each action and everyday activity—talking, cooking, having a shower, making love, or commuting to work. Accepting yourself means rejoicing in everything, including each person who comes into your life, because your life receives a new dimension and becomes a poem.

3.6 How to heal your heart

The deepest healings are those when you feel and become aware of something by yourself.

This is an important topic for the entirety of humanity, because we carry our emotions in our emotional heart. We carry all disappointments in love, feelings of being unloved, abandoned, all hurt, pain, and suffering in our heart. This is where we store it all. People are often unaware that they are doing this; they are not aware of their deeply suppressed feelings. This often happens to men, who were taught not to show their feelings. But it happens to women as well.

It all begins in early childhood, even in the fetal period. As small children, we felt our mother's and father's feelings, their disappointments in love. Later on, we also received the feeling that we weren't given enough attention. A child will receive those feelings from different situations, they don't need to be "catastrophic" traumas. If a child is left in a place they don't want to be, at their grandparents', in a nursery or hospital, they will create the feelings of being unloved, abandoned, unwanted, lonely, unworthy of their mother's love. This will also happen in situations when you promise something and don't fulfill your promise, or when you give something to their siblings, but not to them, or when you tell a lie in front of your child. Those are all traumas for a child. They don't know what is happening. All of those situations result in feelings of not being worthy, not being good enough, not deserving their mother's and father's love. That influences all areas of a child's life.

In relationship with the parents, the child creates the feeling of worthiness. If that feeling is not there, the child feels that they don't deserve their parents' love, good things, good relationships, good financial situations, and work. That is why it is so important to know how to attain the feeling of worthiness, how to feel a mother's and father's love. It is important to see what was really happening in that relationship and realize that a child's perception of that is often limited, and it is not the highest truth. The highest truth is that they loved you (the child) the best that they knew and could. Many parents didn't learn how to be conscious parents. They didn't know better. They did as they were shown by their parents, and what others did. They often didn't agree with your perspective. As a child, we don't see the whole picture; we only see our own needs. Later on, as adults, that continues—we often see only how we feel. We often don't think about how others feel in their own skin; we often don't consider why somebody didn't do what we expected.

We need a broader, intuitive insight in order to overcome those situations and heal ourselves. Ask to be shown that—ask the energy of creation, the highest consciousness or intelligence within yourself to show you what really happened, why your parents treated you as they did, and what was happening in their lives at the time. Then focus on your heart, on your heart chakra, and you will receive messages in the form of an image, insight, or as a voice you hear. You just need to ask the higher consciousness, higher wisdom, and intelligence to tell you and show you why your mother and father behaved as they did, and what they felt for you in their hearts. This will bring you huge relief and opportunity to feel the great love they had in their hearts. It is not enough just to talk about that love.

The best and deepest healings are those where you feel something and become aware of it by yourself. Things that you personally become aware of in your life will stay with you. My wish is to share these healings with you, to help you heal your heart so you can feel loved, first by your mother and father, and then by the universe. The whole universe loves you, but it is best to start from your mother and father, because they are the ones who shaped you and influenced so many things in your life.

3.7 How to heal the physical body

There are feelings in our inner bodies that need to be healed, harmonized, and balanced.

The physical body suffers because of the negative feelings and toxins that attach to those feelings. It is very important to know which feelings you should work on, because we are not aware of all of our feelings. I believe that feelings and beliefs cause the problems and diseases we have. I believe if we have carried those feelings for many years, a disease will appear. Those feelings produce chemicals which attack our bodies and destroy our DNA. Toxins also destroy our bodies, but we are often not aware of what is happening. When we work on ourselves, it is often superficial. We carry deeply suppressed feelings in our bodies, in our cells and DNA. Once we get in touch with those feelings, we can heal them. When we become aware of them, we can transform them into higher consciousness. When this healing happens, it happens through the intelligence of our body. Our own consciousness is healing us through the inner koshas.

An example of using body intelligence is when we are aware of our body, and we become aware of the feelings inside of the body. A portal will open in our body, like an inner world. Then we use the inner intelligence of our body to facilitate healing. We ask ourselves what kind of message that problem has for us.

Another way of healing physical and emotional problems is through God's grace, or grace of the universe, which descends upon us when we ask for it. It descends upon us in hopeless situations. Grace can heal any disease. God's grace is a gift from heaven; it is independent of the laws of the universe, because it overrides them. God, in his compassion, sends grace and heals us when we pray for it, or even without our prayers.

People used to think that you need to do penance and renunciation to earn God's grace. Some people believed that, so that was true for them. However, grace can descend even without penance. If the results or the healing we are looking for do not come, it is because the person is not open enough to receiving grace into their life, or they are refusing healing in some way. Grace is life itself; everything that happens to us is God's grace and everything happens through grace. Bad things are also a gift from heaven. That is the truth we need to accept into our lives. When we are lonely, when we have or don't have a happy family, kids, a wonderful spouse, when we have or don't have any money, all of it is God's grace. This is the truth we need to accept. When we believe in that truth, there is a feeling of humbleness and respect for all creation.

If we don't want to pray, we can ask for grace to descend on us or on another person. Grace can cleanse the aura, heal chakras, relieve pain or solve any other problem. We can also ask for protection. We can ask for grace to descend any time we want. It is a gift from God.

3.8 How to heal the fetal period

Everything that parents carry within will reflect on the health of the fetus and its future life.

Our fetal period is very important for our life. The fetus is alive; it is teeming with life energy; it hears and perceives everything in its environment. Each moment of this period leaves a trace on the fetus and the future child. Many of the latter life patterns, events and behavioral patterns depend on the fetal period. The fetus feels its mother and father, as well as other close people around. At the moment of conception, the parents may not have yet decided to have a child, perhaps they didn't want a child, or it was a case of abuse. The fetus takes on these feelings.

The moment when the mother told the father she was pregnant influences the fetus. Sometimes a twin sibling will not survive the pregnancy, and the surviving sibling will feel guilty. When we leave the womb, we continue to take on lots of stuff from our mother and father.

In the fetal period, but also during childhood, self-confidence and feeling of worthiness are built. People often lack the feeling of being worthy. They would like to create many things in their lives, but they don't feel worthy of them. Feeling worthy starts forming in the mother's womb, and then later in the first four years of life. If the relationship between mother and father was full of problems and fighting, the fetus will absorb those problems. Addictions to alcohol, cigarettes, and drugs reflect on the fetus' nervous system. If the parents were drinking or taking drugs, it will reflect on the child's brain and behavior. If the parents' relationship is problematic and full of dramatic situations, the child will develop insecurities and have no self-confidence. The child develops a feeling that they are in a dead-end situation, trapped in the relationship with the mother and father. This will repeat later in life as a pattern from the past. The child feels threatened and not welcome in the world. Viruses and other harmful microorganisms can influence the physical and mental health of the fetus and can cause numerous diseases and disorders. Different kinds of damage to the brain may occur.

Birth is the key moment in forming our perception of life and future life events. Researchers are starting to discover that the degree to which a human birth was difficult or traumatic will influence the amount of hardship in that person's life. It can be especially traumatic if the child is born by cesarean section. If the child doesn't have enough air to breathe, they can live with feeling a certain heaviness throughout their whole life, or they can have feelings of suffocating and suffer from respiratory system disorders. It is necessary to resolve all those traumas and feelings from the fetal period. These traumas are healed by healing each moment from conception to birth.

Humans have the potential to heal no matter how traumatic their birth experience was.

Exercise. Healing the Fetal Period

> You need to ask to become aware of the feelings you received at the time of conception, when your mother told your father she was expecting, when you lost a twin sibling, or at the moment of birth. Ask the highest consciousness within you to show you yourself as a fetus and feel how this fetus felt. Put all those feelings in the bag and do the True Acceptance 1 exercise from Chapter 2. You can also use the Direct Method exercise in Chapter 2. Find the feelings of being cherished, accepted, cared for, and looked after. Ask yourself how you would feel if you were loved by your mother and father, if you were a happy baby in your mother's womb.

We are looking for feelings of happiness, enthusiasm, and respect for life. Then find those feelings in your body and spread them through the whole body. In the end, ground yourself. Another way is to imagine that little fetus and send it your love until you change its unpleasant feelings. You are sending the child the message that they are loved, accepted and safe. Repeat this until the child gets the feeling they are welcome to this world. This healing will reflect in all areas of your life.

Our relationship with our father will influence a child's spiritual growth, healing work, progress, development, and their relationship with God. While the child is in the womb, and later as well, the child doesn't differentiate between their father and God. The most important thing is to heal all traumas from the period of conception to birth. You need to forgive, because forgiving is the best healing. You need to understand and accept that your mother and father did the best they knew, and it is not your fault. There is a reason why you chose such a mother and father, why you chose that particular genetic line.

Once we forgive, we are free even from the laws of the universe, which then have no influence on us. When we forgive, our life moves in a different direction, because forgiveness influences our behavior and inclinations.

3.9   How to heal your inner child

We carry joy within but have lost touch with it.

Our inner child is the child we actually used to be, and we still carry it within us. It is a child that feels joy and playfulness, that is delighted by pure being, just being here, being able to communicate, to exist and move around. Children are happy with little things. This is something children know, and adults need to learn. What holds us back in life and development is the constant striving for something, believing we lack something, and not seeing the little things, not enjoying them and not being grateful for them. A child enjoys everything; it is content and has inner joy and connection with the source of joy within. We have lost touch with that delight, that celebration of life.

That happened to us because we took on the entire story from our parents, their emotions, because our subconsciousness absorbed their truth. We absorbed it when we were still fetuses, we have been absorbing it since birth. We have accumulated layers of beliefs, feelings, attitudes, and opinions belonging to others, which now prevent this inner joy from coming to the light of day. All those artificial layers were not here the whole time. Just as they came, just as we adopted those group fears and feelings of our nations and ancestors, so can we release them.

When we take something on from others, it has its place and the reason why it is there. We need to dive deeper into our nature, until we reach that source of celebration of life. That joyful child is our true being we carry within. Be present in each moment. It doesn't mean you will never get sad, but you can always return to that source that is always within us. Once we become aware of that joy, nobody can take it away from us.

෬ Exercise. Connect to Your Inner Child

Let me guide you through a simple meditation. Start by asking yourself: "If I truly accepted the joy of life, enjoying each moment, everything that is happening around me, how would I feel?" Write down feelings that come in answer to this question. Would you feel thrilled, complete, safe, happy, or joyful?

When you find what those feelings would be, in that way you discover and become aware of some new levels of your being. If you could feel those feelings in some part of your body, ask yourself where that would be. You can feel them in your belly, neck, chest. Then you need to find those feelings inside yourself, in your body. We can discover some new feelings in our bodies, that we were not aware of before, like sadness, grief, anger, rage, or disappointment. You need to let those feelings just be there.

Then we go deeper and deeper into our own being and ask the highest consciousness within us to feel that joy of life, the joy of existence. We can now feel that ecstasy of being, joy, love, and playfulness. Now become aware of those feelings in the body, and ask them to spread through the whole body, through your heart and soul, blood, and DNA. Slowly observe what is happening in your body.

If you have any problems during this process, ask the highest consciousness to make those feelings stronger, more intense. Once you feel them in each cell of your body, you will know that you are that child. Be present with each feeling. Accept that as a part of your being and know that you can always return there; this is you and this is your true nature. When you feel all that, thank

> God for this healing, thank your soul family, ancestors, laws of the universe. Say: "I accept my inner child. I deserve healing. I accept the support of my soul family, ancestors and laws of the universe." Imagine roots coming out of your body, through your feet, going into the earth, 100 meters down and 100 meters to the sides. You can always return to your inner child any time you wish.

3.10 How to heal your soul

We have all the knowledge within us, but we need life experience to return us to that knowledge so that we become aware of it.

Our soul has its own being, its individuality, its personality. The soul evolves, just like we evolve. Although the soul is strong, powerful, and divine—an aspect of universal consciousness—it still needs help to evolve. It is important to understand that we need to heal the moment when the soul was separated from the divine consciousness. This is the moment when the soul first felt loneliness and being abandoned. It is the moment when it lost its home, its identity, when it became separated from existence, and it lost itself. This feeling of separation has been with us throughout our entire lives. We often start various adventures, jobs, and relationships, or even look for this unity in sex, drugs, alcohol, in other people and places. But we cannot find it there.

We look for the original unity the soul lost during the separation from the energy of unconditional love, or God. It did not happen without consent; it was an act of love, just like the birth of a child is an act of love. This act of love is traumatic for the baby because it is entering a new reality; it is leaving the beauty and warmth of its home—the mother's womb—and going out into a completely new world.

The separation of the soul is just as traumatic. It is a natural process, because the universe evolves in that way. Through development of souls, the consciousness expands, and the universe prospers. The separation happened because we need duality to experience the original unity again, to experience love. Without the world, the universal consciousness cannot experience the love it carries. The souls were created to multiply and spread this love. Through this love, the universal principle experiences itself. We have all the knowledge within us, but we need life experience to return us to that knowledge, so that we become aware of it.

Our evolutionary path is similar to the evolutionary path of the soul. This evolution is needed to manifest love and accept it as the highest reality. There is no greater reality than the universal love, which reigns and waits to be realized through our souls. Our whole life is a game that leads us to that realization. The trauma of birth causes the feeling of separation. Just as it is important to heal the fetus' traumas, it is important to heal the traumas of the soul. This is how we return to the Garden of Eden.

Everybody needs this healing because it helps us better understand our lives and reality. When we understand everything we have done in our lives, we won't yearn for things that cannot give us the feeling of fulfillment. This feeling can be achieved only through unity with the entire existence. The soul has accepted its evolutionary path through suffering, pain, lack of love, remorse, regret, dissatisfaction, and lack of money. It needs to be given a possibility to evolve through abundance, contentment, joy, and love. That will affect change in our life.

The soul creates our life because it is a force of enormous power. If the soul carries unresolved traumas and has accepted that it must grow through suffering, pain, misunderstanding, lack of love and abundance, those things will manifest in our lives. We then wonder why those things are happening to us.

The soul is an enormous potential that needs to develop within us. We need to change its path of evolution and changes will be obvious in our lives. We need to discover which qualities we need, but haven't developed, that would help us integrate the soul completely into our bodies. The more the soul enters the body, the greater our feelings of richness of life and contentment. This is a great healing that everybody needs. In order to enter the next phase of our evolution, we need to develop the soul and revive the unity of existence of universal love, happiness, and contentment.

3.11 How to make contact with your soul

Ask your soul whether it is satisfied with its life.

It is important to make contact with your soul, to accept it and become aware of it, to connect with it, understand it, and to see how it feels and what it wants.

ℰ Exercise. Make Contact with Your Soul

Sit down or lay down and make yourself comfortable and relax. Close your eyes and turn inwards; connect with your inner being. Focus on your inner body and how it feels. Ask the source within you, the highest consciousness, God within you: "God, connect me with my soul, so I can see it and communicate with it."

Visualize a light in front of your third eye (in the middle of your forehead). This is the light of your soul. It can be one meter in front of you, or less. Feel this light of the soul entering your body, and when you feel it, you will be infused with great peace. This is the sign that you have connected with your soul, that you have felt it. Silently, talk to your soul and ask it how it feels, what message it wants to give you for your life.

Once you've become aware of that, ask it what is important for its development, what is happening with it, what it would like you to do or change in your life. Ask your soul whether it is satisfied with its life. Ask it to accept you into its life. Tell your soul that you accept it, too, that you want it to be present within you as much as possible, and that you want to act from the depths of your soul. Tell your soul it can manifest through you and realize its wishes.

When you have done that, say goodbye to your soul and return to your body. Thank your soul. You can ask your soul for advice on anything that is troubling you in your life.

❧ Exercise. Healing the Separation of the Soul

The next exercise is for healing the separation of the soul, the moment when we were separated from the whole, or the moment of exile from the Garden of Eden. Now is the time to return to that unity. In this exercise we resolve the birth trauma, that is, our separation from the universal consciousness. Once again, we will connect with our inner selves.

Relax; observe your body and what it feels. Ask the energy of life, or the highest consciousness within you to show you the moment of creation of your soul, and how the soul felt at that moment. Focus on your body or on the third eye and you will see the moment of creation of your soul, how your soul separated and how it felt at the time. Most often the soul will feel fear, separation, and rejection. There are also the feelings of helplessness and being lost.

Ask the highest consciousness to show you why all that happened and why your soul felt that way. Ask to be shown the highest truth. You should see that it was an act of God's love for you, as a part of a higher plan for evolution of souls and the universe. This realization that everything is all right and that you are taken care of brings about healing of all those feelings.

In that moment you should feel the unity of existence, like you are coming home to yourself. If those feelings are not released, you need to do the Transformation of Consciousness exercise until you become aware of the complete unity of existence, of your having returned home. Ground yourself again and give thanks for the healing. Thank the energy of creation and do the grounding like we did in the previous exercises. This exercise will bring you back to the original reality and revive the memory of being connected with the entire universe. This will balance your ego and bring balance into your life.

☙ Exercise. Heal the Evolutionary Path of the Soul

This exercise is for healing the evolutionary path of the soul. The soul has chosen to evolve through a certain path. Usually after a difficult birth we also choose a dramatic evolutionary path. Maybe we will have financial difficulties or challenging relationships. Now is the moment to change this developmental path.

Become aware of your body and your inner self. Ask your being, this divine consciousness within you, to show you the moment of creation of your soul. Focus on your third eye and you will see that moment. Ask the energy of creation to change the evolutionary path of the soul and ask it to release all vows, obligations, contracts, agreements of the soul, and to evolve through suffering, sadness, fear, unforgiveness, drama, lack of money, love and contentment, disease or any other lack you may feel in your life. The goal is to give the soul instructions so it will know how to evolve through success, love, understanding, cooperation, togetherness with others, good relationship with yourself, and self-love.

Witness those changes. This is done in the identity, in the very core of the soul. We release the old and ask the energy of creation to give the soul a new way of evolution through love. Witness this process. When all the old energy has gone, we will take the soul to the seventh plane of existence, or pure consciousness. Ask God or the energy of creation to take the soul into pure consciousness, the energy of unconditional divine love. Visualize taking the soul higher and higher, until you feel this energy of unconditional divine love.

Ask God, the energy of creation, to once again change everything you have witnessed changing, to enable the soul to have a new evolutionary path and do all of that in the energy of the seventh plane of existence. When this is done, ask the soul once again to descend and integrate into your body. You will feel it entering more and more into you. Tell the God inside of you that you feel comfortable, that you accept this change in your whole body, in everything you are, in your blood, your DNA, in your whole self. Ask the energy of creation to teach the soul to know who it is without all those things you have just released, to know its purpose and identity without its former self. Then ask it to teach you all those things as well.

Exercise. Descending of the Soul into the Body

The following exercise is also useful to make contact with your soul. Take a pen and paper. Ask your soul what you need to embrace it in your life, which energies, and knowledge, so that it can fully integrate into your life and stay with you. The soul is present in your body up to eighty per cent. The higher its presence, it is a sign of unity with existence, showing that our vibration is at the highest level. We will feel merging, like we have been given a new life. When we lead a life that is not harmonized with our soul, the soul, with its energy and creation, is less and less present in our life. This happens because life runs its own course, so it is necessary to align with the soul.

When we complete this exercise, we will see how much power, joy, love, and inspiration we can feel. Connect with your soul like you did in the first exercise and ask it what it needs to integrate fully. When the soul gives you an answer, look for those qualities within yourself, in some part of your body, until you find them. Go deep inside your being until you feel them. That can be joy, courage, compassion, contentment, honesty, depending on what you need. You need to go deeper within until you feel those qualities, and then spread them throughout your whole body. Finally, you need to ground yourself and say thanks. You will feel the soul descending more and more, and you will become increasingly powerful, more stable, and creative.

3.12 Do we need to heal ourselves first before healing others?

It is natural to have our own issues that frustrate us, that are still unresolved and blocking us.

This topic is interesting both for healers and their clients. There is a common misconception that a healer should not have any issues of their own. It is a part of human nature to have imperfections and weaknesses. It is natural to have our own issues that frustrate us, that are still unresolved and blocking us. The same goes for healers and people who work on themselves. They are all human. Healers also have their own issues, areas of life that need to be worked on and balanced. They also need advice and help from their friends or other healers.

It is more difficult to help yourself with your own issues. We are less focused on our own unresolved stuff because it is easier to spot those things in others. For most healers it is much easier to detect other people's issues than their own. Healers also need advice, and they are just as imperfect as any other person. They have their own life paths and purpose. So it is a great misconception to expect people on a spiritual path to not have any problems. In such situations, they are forced to present themselves as perfect, without any problems. On the one hand we have the public expecting those people to be perfect, and on the other hand we have healers falsely presenting themselves. This false narrative does not serve society, healers, or their clients.

The sooner we accept our imperfect nature as a part of evolution and progress, a part of life, the closer we come to self-realization and achieving our goals, living in abundance, happiness, and fulfillment. All therapists, healers and people on a spiritual path grow and develop. The more we work on ourselves, the more we can help others. This work is necessary for the development of society. There are people who don't need healing, who have a healthy nature, whose lives are not dominated by their egos. Those are the people who accept life, who are ready to help others in trouble. They don't need to belong to any spiritual movement; they are healthy people who feel connection to others and understand that we share common unresolved issues. They accept themselves, rejoice in life, are dedicated to what they do. Not everybody needs to go to see a therapist or a healer. If you are looking for help, don't expect perfect and ideal people who will help you. Everybody is on their own path of evolution, just like the universe that keeps evolving. The whole universe is expanding. Everything is growing and developing. Progress is in the very core of the soul and the universe.

We all live under the same sky, on the same planet, sharing the same being that manifests through us. There is beauty in having your own individuality and being a part of a whole. This is the beauty of existence.

CHAPTER 4

Living with purpose

4.1 How to live with happiness and purpose

The moment has come for us to move from fear into the beauty of our inner being, into joy, peace, and happiness.

There are plans on this Earth to keep people in fear and manipulate them, and this is not happening for the first time in history. Throughout contemporary and older history people have been scared of different diseases, political leaders, and nations. In that way they were sent to war, intimidated, and were easy to manipulate. The last such incident was the Covid-19 pandemic with everything that accompanied it, then the wars that are currently being fought in the world. However, behind it all is a greater plan of the universe for people to realize they should start taking care of each other, realize that we are all part of a big family, and that you cannot do harm to others and expect good things for yourself.

Might this be the time for people to finally wake up, to finally bring back the purpose and meaning to life? Perhaps the time has come for people to say their lives are beautiful, that they are responsible for their lives, for themselves, to love their lives, help themselves and others grow and progress, feel love and understanding for themselves, others, and the entire planet. Maybe now is the moment to feel that we need to live in fullness and purpose, because through our growth we contribute to the growth of all humanity.

The moment has come for us to move from fear into the beauty of our inner being, into joy, peace, and happiness. This happiness is not outside of ourselves; it is within us and this highest consciousness is waiting to be manifested through us, to develop and speak through us. I believe that now is the right moment, and everything that is happening is good and positive for us, although it doesn't seem so at first.

4.2 How to move forward with our growth

It is never too late to spread our wings and make our dreams come true.

Nowadays, we identify personal growth with the number of books someone has read, classes and schools they have completed, or affiliations with certain spiritual groups. Personal growth is actually progress in our daily life, noticeable in our feelings and reactions to the world. Maybe our life hasn't been the easiest, or we haven't chosen an easy life path, but everything that has happened has its meaning and importance. If we could see the whole picture, our reactions and feelings would be much more positive, brighter, or optimistic. We would know that the universe is working for us, not against us, although it may not seem so at first. We would also know that when we lose something, there is something much better waiting for us. Our soul and our higher self are already creating solutions for our life challenges. It is never too late to make our dreams come true, spread our wings and soar like eagles, looking at the world from above, from God's perspective.

This world is God's world. I will not hesitate to use the word God or replace it with "the present moment" or something similar. Simply put, this word for me represents love and omnipresence, omnipotence, and omniscience. Other words that I use here with the same meaning are: source, energy of creation, highest consciousness or intelligence, life energy. When I say this is God's world, I mean that this love and consciousness is within us, around us, in others, in our every thought, deed and feeling, because everything is divine. This love or consciousness is the basis for everything else; everything emanates from it and returns to it. We are all gods walking around in human bodies, not knowing it, thinking that God is somewhere far away or very difficult to reach, that it takes many years of work to receive God's love and affection. The truth is the complete opposite—we have never been separated from God, nor will we ever be.

Separation from God is suffering, pain and sorrow, and unity with God is the joy of life, joy of existence, and celebration of the whole of existence. We just need to pay attention to that joy, energy, fullness or God's presence, which is in us and around us. There is nothing else necessary for growth but shifting our focus from our problems, disappointments, feelings of sadness, pain, and insecurity, to this consciousness, energy, and life. We can call it any name we like; it is what it is, what it has always been and always will be, what gives us life and breath, heartbeat, thoughts, feelings, everything we have, what supports us and loves us.

It is crucial to see that we already have the love we have been looking for our whole life, that everything is soaked in love, that we are swimming in the sea of love just like fish swim in the ocean. It is important to feel that joy and happiness we can return to when we are sad and unhappy. Happiness is our nature, and we can choose to be happy. This is a developmental step that we are asked to take. We don't need to wait for happiness to come when we achieve or accomplish something. The things we have achieved or accomplished can only strengthen the feeling of happiness and contentment that is already within us.

There are two important things that lead to realization or awareness of happiness. The first one is forgiveness, and the second is gratitude. Those are the greatest secrets of the universe. They are stronger even than the laws that govern this universe. Although this might sound pretentious, I still believe it is close to the truth. The more gratitude we have, the stronger and more developed we are; we walk the paths of God or the paths of truth, of understanding and acceptance of self, the world, and God.

Gratitude and forgiveness are different sides of the same coin. True forgiveness means being grateful for everything, including any resentment we feel toward ourselves and others. We can be grateful that those people came into our lives.

It is important to be grateful for all the so-called flaws and imperfections we have accused ourselves of, for existence, life, the air that we breathe, eyes and ears that enable us to see and hear, for the opportunity to love and rejoice in life. Gratitude and forgiveness mean that there is a higher meaning of everything, a higher truth, God, or source that is taking care of us; there is justice and laws that govern this world. It means we have a deep respect for all creation, and we are in harmony with the laws of the universe.

In order to forgive, we first need to understand the other person and understand ourselves—why we (or they) did what we (or they) did, or why we (or they) didn't do what we wanted. The easiest way to understand that is to ask the highest consciousness or life energy within us to show us what was happening in our life (or the life of the person) when we (or they) acted in a certain way. To do this, we need to go out of our own paradigm and enter our (or the other person's) reality. After understanding, we need to accept that everything that happened was supposed to happen, that both we and the other person did the best we knew and could in that moment.

Understanding ourselves and others leads to transformation of consciousness or broadening our perspective. God forgives and accepts us and the world we live in, because he sees the truth—that everything happens for a reason. The truth is that our choices create our reality, so the healthiest thing to do is accept everything that is happening with understanding, without struggle. In the end, you will feel there was really nothing to forgive, and everything is okay. Great and powerful souls forgive. That is not weakness or powerlessness. To forgive does not mean to let somebody control you; it is not giving away your power to others. On the contrary, this is how you remain in your power.

4.3 How to find your deepest inner being

The goal is to live in the eternity of existence, making decisions and creating our lives from that being.

The total of our being consists of our feelings, thoughts, identifications, possessions, our body, thinking, viewpoints, personality, soul, heart, ego, emotional, mental, and astral bodies. When we say "I", all of that is included. We wonder what is really the "I" when we say, "my body, thoughts or feelings", when we say that we have a beautiful partner, house, or bank account. Who is the "I" that has all that? What is the nature of that "I", or what is meant by that "I"? Obviously, that "I" is separated from our thoughts, feelings, bodies, and possessions. When you ask somebody how they are, they will say: "I'm fine", or that they're angry, sick, or happy. Our states change, but the "I" remains the same.

You have always had it—as a child and now as an adult, you have the same "I". Whatever happens in the future, the same "I" will be involved, whether you are healthy, happy, or sick, the "I" is always the same. The same consciousness was present when you were three years old, and now as you are reading this book. The same consciousness or "I" is reading these lines. You might think you are very much different from your three-year-old self, but what is it that is different in you—your "I" or your thoughts, feelings, personality, or body? Or is your consciousness the same and it is the basis of your experiences?

⁓ Exercise. Know Your True Being

If we want to get to know our highest consciousness or our being, along with the transformation of ego, we ask the energy of creation to show us the very root, the source of our thoughts and feelings, or to show us who that thinking, feeling "I" is.

Ask to be shown who the "I" is, then go deeper and

deeper into it, until you are shown its true nature. At first, you might see the ego as "I", but ego is an artificial creation made of your thoughts, feelings, and past experiences. Ego is an artificial entity created from fears and identifications. It is possible to perceive the ego as a cloud, an entity that is a part of yourself.

Ask yourself who is aware of that ego, and you will see it is an endless, limitless consciousness or life energy, life within you, what you really are.

From that position of consciousness, tell the ego that you accept it, that it is a part of you, that you love it, and it has a significant place in your life. Locate it in your body and ask for the message it wants to give you. For example, the ego may tell you that you are strong, that you can achieve what you want. Feel that strength in your body, in each cell; this strength, or maybe love, is exactly what you need to become aware of your infinite nature, endless or deep peace, fullness of existence. It is a great nothing, but still full and endless, powerful, and gentle at the same time.

After that, make a list and write down everything you mean by "I" and "mine". In other words, write down everything you identify with: your feelings, thoughts, successes, failures, roles as a mother, son, brother, your possessions. Write down the things you think you have: a partner, a bank account, a car. Write down everything that happened to you in the past and how you identified with it: all hurts, wounds, things you haven't forgiven, or healed.

Ask yourself what would happen if you completely let go of all those identifications, what would be left? If you took a step back from everything, feel what would be left—that is your being or consciousness. The next question to ask yourself is: what is the worst thing that would happen if I let go of everything on the list? Keep asking that until you come to the answer that you would become nothing, or you would lose your old identity and become everything—the entire universe.

The purpose of these exercises is detachment from the dominance of ego over you or your true being, from giving too much importance to the identifications of the ego or balancing of the ego. The goal is to enter your own being, or "I", and become fully aware of it. From this position, look at your fears and other problems. They will seem very small, unimportant, insignificant. The objective is the transformation of feelings and ego into your true being, or "I".

If those fears, different feelings, and problems still seem heavy and insurmountable, we use the exercises of True Acceptance and Transformation of Consciousness, in Chapter 2, this time doing them from the position of our true nature. The goal is to live in the eternity of existence, making decisions and creating our lives from that being. The purpose of these exercises is to see through the illusion of existence, to see that nothing is separate from God or our highest consciousness, and the background or basis of everything is the same consciousness or energy. It stands behind the ego and all of its identifications, in the background of all our thoughts, feelings, actions, successes, and failures.

Once again, we see the need to accept and transform all parts of ourselves into the higher or highest consciousness we have within, and live our lives in unity, connection, and love.

4.4 What are the stages of development and who are spiritual teachers?

Be aware of yourself and happiness you carry within; do not trust the misconceptions of the mind that happiness is waiting for us out there, once we get what we want.

Spiritual life is never separated from material life. It is integrated in every aspect. A long time ago, I wanted to live in India, because my spiritual teacher Sri Sathya Sai Baba was incarnated there. My intention was to dedicate my life to Him and be a spiritual person—doing yoga, namasmarana (repeating of God's name), and seva (service to others). All worldly activities, as I used to call them, like work, going out, and my love life, seemed secondary and unimportant at the time. Many people surrounding me used to think the same way. Millions of people were gathering in India, and we were all eagerly awaiting the day and hour when we would be on Indian land again and see our beloved teacher.

Interestingly, Sri Sathya Sai Baba was not interested in such an approach. He would send people home, telling them they should work, get married, and live where they were born, helping their communities develop. They should focus on healthy relationships within their families first, and then go out to communities and help each other grow in life. He was teaching that human values and qualities were true spirituality. According to Him, honesty, truthfulness, righteousness, fairness, love, non-violence, and peace are the basic human qualities and the basis of a healthy life in abundance for the family and community. He used to say we should move from "I" toward "we", to stop being preoccupied just with ourselves, but start thinking about others. That is true development and growth.

Today, many years later, I understand the importance of His words and see that we need to show our qualities in everyday life. The trap of the ego is so powerful that it creates the so-called spiritual ego, which uses ideas of spirituality to avoid working on ourselves and deflects us from the right path and growth.

I am afraid that many young people, as well as older, fall into this trap through different techniques and spiritual schools, thinking they are special, superior to others. It that way they block their development and growth.

But I also think that all spiritual practices people do to purify themselves or their consciousness are important and help development to a certain degree, when the time comes to stand on our own two feet and live the teachings, applying them in our lives. My teacher used to say that hands that help others are more valuable than hours of meditation, or a praying mouth, and that we should be happy with our lives.

Complete wisdom is contained in the words "be happy". Be aware of yourself and the happiness you carry within; do not trust the misconceptions of the mind that happiness is waiting for us out there, once we get what we want. It is also important to love what you do, instead of doing what you love. There is so much wisdom and truth in those few words. If we live according to them, we have already reached our goal. The goal is for everybody to be happy, fulfilled, and healthy, to love their lives, themselves, and existence, and to rejoice in all creation. In other words, people should get out of their heads, ideas, and mental space in everyday life and situations, and connect into their hearts. The inability to receive love, or separation from love is what prevents us from doing that.

This is the same as separation from life and life force. It is the feeling that you are isolated individuals fighting for survival with other ego individuals, accompanied by the feeling of separation from the entire creation, from God, the energy of creation. This is the root of all of our trepidations, worries, and fears. It is important to overcome this separation, the feelings of lack or inadequacy, feeling that we are missing something all the time, of being a victim instead of being in our power.

There are many teachings and teachers today talking about the oneness of existence, or Advaita philosophy, which teaches that we are all one being or consciousness, that we all share the same consciousness or being. Everything that exists is one being, which expresses itself through the material world; God or consciousness permeates everything. Each, even the smallest thing, deserves our respect and admiration, and we deserve the same respect and admiration as well. If we have really accepted that truth, we have come to the point where we began being or existing—to the being or source of everything. Living in that consciousness and being completely present in everyday life is the goal of all spiritual teachings.

In my opinion, all of these Advaita teachings are either not practical—people just meditate on the highest consciousness and lose interest in everyday life—or everything seems fine during meditation, but afterwards, people are again faced with their unresolved life issues, feelings, and traumas that are waiting to be addressed and resolved.

This is why we need to go step by step, resolving all unresolved issues from childhood, then go even further to the fetal period and the pre-fetal period. Metaphorically speaking, it is good to build the house of your life on a sound foundation, not skipping things, looking for quick solutions, or covering issues up.

Of all modern teachers of Advaita philosophy, Rupert Spira is the person who provides complete understanding of the whole story of unity of existence. He is a great inspiration for the development of consciousness and spirituality.

There are different stages in spirituality, but I would say that all of us took the following, or similar, path: "I want to deal with my unresolved issues; I want to be happy and successful in life and in what I do. I want to live my life in the fullness of consciousness, enjoy, be joyful, healthy, release my fears, grudges, worry, and guilt. I want to be relaxed, happy with myself and my existence, live in abundance and have plenty of all things: love, money, material, and spiritual stuff. I want to realize my full potential and abilities." Let's make it happen!

I think that the time has come for new, unwritten chapters in spirituality and healing techniques. More and more, new, quick, efficient techniques for working on yourself and others have been emerging. Many techniques are channeled from "above", directly from the source or highly developed masters from the fifth plane of existence. The reason for this is because the planet has reached a moment in its development that is asking for deep and fast solutions for development and growth.

4.5 What is the purpose of people on this planet?

Purpose is something that fulfills you, makes you happy, inspires you.

We all have our individual purpose, things that are important to us. Those purposes are different—for one person owning a house and land is important; for another it is money, love, being acknowledged and respected, having God's love, or personal development. All those purposes are important for your development and growth, even the material things. Maybe your soul has never felt something, never had such an experience. Our souls develop through experiences. If you need a holiday home or a car for that experience, you will choose such a direction in your life. If you need love, that is what will happen. Those purposes are important for our life and growth, for our existence.

Purpose is something that fulfills you, makes you happy, inspires you. It is something you work on tirelessly, you are completely committed to it, and finally, you achieve it. Purpose is deeper than it seems. It might sometimes look trivial, but purpose comes from the inside, from your inner self, and it pushes you in a particular direction. It may be the calling you feel for your work, your activity, for what you want to achieve. It is an impulse you feel inside, nudging you to take a certain path. Purpose is a deeper level you have come here to achieve. That might be family and kids, helping one person or hundreds of thousands of people. It may be connected to food, having a strong body, or a wish to become healthy again.

A common aspect of humanity is that there is a purpose of development of Earth connected to your personal purpose. It is the need to go very deep into our own being, to realize our divine nature and divine qualities in everyday life, to live the love we have inside, which shows itself through our lives, actions, and feelings. The purpose is to be led through life by that love that connects us, because we all come from the same source. All of humanity is a big family that functions as one. If one person is suffering, another one cannot be happy. If that happens, the family is not functional. The purpose of humanity is common to all, to share the same nature of divine love. This nature is common to all creation—humans, plants, and animals. All of creation is our kin; we are all brothers and sisters. We should nurture such relationships with others—friendly relationships, where we see that we are all parts of one whole. The key is to realize this love through our actions, because in that way we bring ourselves into harmony with the entire existence and the universe—we achieve the harmony of existence. It makes it easier to create, to make decisions; we live our full potential and interact with others through the energy of love. We are not separate individuals but connected with the totality of life. This is the purpose of humanity on a global scale. By fulfilling our individual purpose, we come closer to the purpose of the whole of humanity.

CHAPTER 5

Love and relationships

5.1 How to forgive your parents

Understanding is the basis of forgiveness.

Let's move toward forgiveness for everything that happened between you and your parents. Choose something they did or didn't do, something you cannot forgive or forget, or something you did to them, and they resented it. Choose something that is troubling you in your relationship with your mother and father. Imagine that troubling feeling, your thoughts about them, or some unresolved situation between you. Write it down, then connect to your inner being. The body is a portal through which we come into contact with the highest consciousness within us. Inhale and exhale deeply and ask the highest consciousness why your parents did some of the things that trouble you, what is the highest truth. It is important to focus on your heart chakra. If you do not receive an answer, ask again. If you do not understand the answer, ask for clarification. When you see that higher truth, the higher perspective, it will help you release the resentment and unforgiveness. Acceptance and forgiveness will happen in this way.

Through forgiveness we break free from the chains of dissatisfaction. We forgive for ourselves, because we see the truth. When a person sees the truth, they see there is really nothing to forgive. What we resent is an illusion of the mind that we create ourselves. In that way we create the suffering and dissatisfaction we experience. You need to repeat this exercise several times, until you completely forgive your mother and father. In this way you also heal your parents, the whole genetic line, including your offspring. If you don't do it, your children will resent you like you resent your parents. The resentment will continue in future generations. By forgiving, you are breaking the karmic chain. You are also healing yourself and your soul, because forgiveness is a new beginning. New energy is entering your life, and you have a new chance to create. This can also bring you physical health. This is the inner wisdom and intuition that is helping you. Healing is happening within you, and it is good to give thanks for that gift.

The relationship with your mother and father is crucial for spiritual growth and success in everyday life. If you do the healing work on others, you can be successful in your healing practice. You will be interested in spiritual growth, ready for changes, new ideas, new perspectives on life, development of your consciousness, and perception. It is important for moving forward, working on yourself, and working with others.

All parents love their children deep in their hearts. No matter how they might behave, there is love in their hearts. Parents do the best they know according to their perceptions and beliefs of what raising children should be like. Our perception is often different from theirs. This is normal, because consciousness is growing, and new generations have new perceptions and understanding. It is important to find mutual understanding and support. A child is in a vulnerable situation, because they depend on their parents. The sooner you develop independence, the easier it will be to understand your parents and accept your relationship.

Understanding is the basis for forgiveness. Without understanding we cannot forgive ourselves or them. Forgiving your parents is a great healing for you and your life. It will make you free of all resentment and open you to new possibilities and perspectives, to better relationships, health, and finances. Forgiveness is great healing for your parents, for you, and the whole genetic line. In that way you enable your children to not resent themselves. Forgiveness brings many blessings into your life.

5.2 Why do we look for love outside of ourselves?

The universe is sending us a message that it loves and accepts us, and we deserve that love.

The reason why our hearts are suffering is the human tendency to look for love outside of ourselves, in other people. We expect other people to fill our hearts and our love lives. We expect them to respond to our need for love. We expect to find the right person who will do it for us. Other people have their own problems; they expect the same from you, so conflicts and misunderstanding are inevitable. What we expect from others and what they expect from us cannot be fulfilled. We are actually looking for healing of old wounds in our hearts. We are searching for someone to heal those wounds, but the other person also has their own wounds they want to heal. We are asking them to do the impossible because they are also searching for love and their hearts are empty.

Our beliefs about love are built on wrong foundations. We already have that love in our hearts, but nobody has ever told us that it is there and that we should look for it inside of ourselves. Pure love, to be loved as we are, with all our qualities and faults is real, true love. When we accept the other person in that way, that is love. We already have that kind of love all around us. We are loved like that by the sky, the moon, the sun, the trees, nature, all beings, the whole universe, and the energy of creation. They are all sending us love. This energy of love is in the very air that we breathe, in prana, in the energy that surrounds us. The universe is constantly sending us a message that it loves and accepts us, and we deserve that love. We can recognize and keep that energy. We can feel that source within ourselves.

What I need to emphasize here is that our hearts are very good at giving love but are not good at receiving it. Most people have an open front heart chakra, but their back heart chakra is closed. Chakras are our energy centers. Many of us feel love for another person but are unable to receive that love in return. Back chakras are in charge of receiving energy from the universe and they are often blocked. It is not just the heart chakra, other back chakras are also blocked, and that is why we have problems in those parts of the body. We are not able to receive love because of something that happened in childhood that closed our chakras down. Even if somebody shows us love, we are not able to receive it.

Exercise. Receive Love: Unblock Your Back Chakra

This exercise, which I received from spiritual teacher Ramaji from the USA, will unblock your back chakras, and fill you with love.

Imagine that you are swimming in a sea of love surrounding you from all sides, like a fish in the ocean. Your body is immersed in that sea. With every inbreath, imagine breathing in that sea of love, breathing in happiness. Hold your breath for a few seconds. Say to yourself: "I am filled with love and happiness." Feel that love and happiness filling you. Stay like that for five to ten seconds.

When you feel you are full of love, breathe out. Feel yourself filling with love from the inside. Say to yourself: "Let me be happy, let me be loved." You can repeat this cycle five times, or as much as you need, until you feel that love and happiness are present within you all the time, that you are no longer missing it. Imagine that love entering not only through your breath, but also through your back chakras, especially the heart chakra. Your chakras are opening, and love is entering your body. Keep that energy in your body for five to ten seconds until you feel you are completely filled with love and happiness. Feel the universe filling you with love. You should enjoy doing this; it is a natural process. If needed, force yourself until it becomes spontaneous and natural.

> The more you do it, the more your chakras will unblock, and you will be able to feel the love of the universe at any time. There will be no more place for disappointment in your heart, because you will stop expecting to receive love and attention from others. We always have love, and we can share it, give it to others. We don't need to expect to receive it from others. By sharing, the love will grow, as will the feeling of fulfillment. It can heal all our love relationships. It will help us to truly live love. We will feel that we are the ones who should give love. We often believe that by giving and not receiving we are weakened. The universe is growing through giving. This is how our hearts and lives are healed.

5.3 How to live universal love

Love is a healing force.

One of the most remarkable ways to heal our hearts is to find love inside of ourselves, the love that we all have, that will fill our hearts, and each cell of our bodies. Love is the greatest reality of our universe. It is pure, selfless love that we have for existence, for ourselves, life, and God.

We all have that love, but we think that we don't. We haven't been taught that we have love inside. Perhaps the moment has come to recognize it. Love is a healing force. It brings happiness and joy. Love has many different aspects. It is not just a feeling; it is existence. Love brings different qualities: peace, contentment, forgiveness, understanding, acceptance, compassion, tolerance. All of those are qualities of love.

We need to understand and accept that true love should be shown through words and actions. It should be love in action. All that love that we feel should manifest in our everyday life and show itself in our thoughts, feelings, words, and deeds. Love needs to come to the light of day. It shouldn't just remain in our heads, as a theory, which is what happens most often. Real love is shown in action, and then we live our true and divine nature, our being. This love comes from the deepest parts of our being, and it is universal. It is one love that connects us all; we are parts of a great being called love. This same love manifests in different ways: in partnerships, friendships, and relationships with our colleagues. In this love there is kindness, forgiveness, but also courage.

If you want to find love, ask yourself how you would feel if you always had the love that you want, if you were fulfilled, and experienced your life through this love, living it every day. Imagine how you would feel. Would you be fulfilled and complete, full of enthusiasm, eagerness, invigoration, and motivation for life? Would you create something great, be an instrument playing music, directed by God's hands?

❦ Exercise. Feel Universal Love

> Ask yourself where you would feel that joy and enthusiasm in your body. You can feel it in any part of the body. The next step is to recognize that love and feelings in the body. Focus on that particular body part. If you feel fear, sadness, anger, or other unpleasant feelings, ask to be taken deeper, until you find love. If you find this difficult, ask the highest intelligence within you, energy of creation or source within you, to take you deeper into your being until you find love.
>
> When you feel that love, ask the feeling to spread through your whole body so you can feel it in every cell. All your cells are filled with love. When you become aware of that, just stay in that energy. If you have difficulties remembering or becoming aware of that, ask the source within you to increase the intensity of those feelings, make them stronger so you can feel them more intensely. You will feel love and accompanying feelings very strongly. Just stay in that feeling, rest within yourself

until all your cells are immersed in that love.

Once you are anchored in that consciousness, when you have accepted it in your life, as your being, you will say thanks for the healing. This is the healing people have been waiting and praying for after years of hard spiritual work, prayer, or discipline. Say thank you to love, to the laws. Say that you are worthy and have support from your ancestors, soul family, and the laws of the universe. Say: "Thank you, thank you, thank you, all." Then ground yourself, imagining roots coming out of your feet and going 100 meters deep into the earth and 100 meters on the sides. You are deeply grounded and feel comfortable.

5.4 How to use truth to solve your problems

*Once we recognize the treasure we have within,
we have reached the end of the journey.*

It is easy to say we shouldn't worry, and it sounds nice, but people will give you a strange look if you say it. We can tell people to say thanks for their lives, but there are people who only think about their difficulties and are not in the mood to be thankful. If we can be truly thankful and trust, that will lead to healing. It is important to see your problem from a broader perspective. You need to see why things happen. Everybody is able to see and hear the truth. We ask the energy of creation or God within us to show us the truth.

For example, if you have just ended a relationship and don't understand why that happened, you can ask the highest intelligence within you to tell you why. Focus on your heart area, on your solar plexus or the third eye in the middle of your forehead, and you will receive the answer. If you are looking for knowledge, you need to go into your heart. If you are looking for a feeling, focus on your solar plexus. If you are clairvoyant—able to see and hear things other people cannot, having ideas beyond the time you live in—then focus on your third eye.

The most important thing is to focus on the energy within you to show you the answer. If you suffer from a disease, or you are entering a business venture, you can ask to be shown the highest truth about it. You can ask if the place you live in is good for you—just ask to be shown the truth. When you see the truth, your problem stops being a problem. This broader perspective that is shown to us, wisdom that is our own, creates lightness of life. We are asking our intuition to show us the truth. It comes from our divine part; the answers come from our own consciousness. If you don't understand or cannot comprehend something, ask to be shown it, or have it clarified, to be shown alternatives, or other possibilities for your growth or development. Ask whether you need to stay on the same path or look for another.

When we ask for a solution, our problems become just creations in our heads. We give power to those problems, but if you give your trust to the higher consciousness or intelligence within you, you will see new, different options that exist in the universe. The problems we have encourage us to dive deeper within ourselves. Everything that is happening to us is guiding us deeper within. In that way we come into deeper contact with our true selves, we start to know our own being.

We are often pestered by new problems and unresolved issues. Their most important purpose is to lead us deep inside, so that we go deep into ourselves, discover our worth, become aware of the inherently worthy beings we are. We are not defined by the things we have done or achieved. Our worth is invaluable. Once we recognize the treasure we have within, we have reached the end of the journey. Then all our problems seem like a breeze that doesn't even touch us. They are no longer problems; just stuff we encounter in life that comes and goes. Those situations are no longer insurmountable and painful because we have found ourselves. When we find ourselves, we realize how much we were looking for ourselves in others, looking for things they cannot give us.

Our purpose is to be in harmony with life and the universe; then spontaneous manifestations and creations will happen. We enter the unity of existence. We see and recognize ourselves in everything. We feel that connection and feel that our life is worthy of living and the best things we can experience on this planet, like happiness, growth, and development.

5.5 How to set healthy boundaries in relationships with others

Healthy relationships with others depend on healthy relationships with ourselves.

This is an issue that bothers many people. The basis for having healthy boundaries with others, where we don't enter other people's space and they don't enter ours, and we are responsible for our lives, is to respect ourselves. Self-respect depends on how much we accept ourseves and how happy we are with ourseves and our life. It is important to accept all our flaws and all of our virtues. If we allow ourselves to be what we are, to express the wishes of our hearts, then we will respect our own lives and personalities, all that we are. When we respect that, the natural course of events is not to let others enter our space too much and hurt us. We will not do things we don't want to, be coerced, controlled, or forced to stay in a relationship we don't want to be in.

The fundamental thing is to be capable of expressing what we are, to accept our inner being, who we are, and feel safe to express that. It is important to respect yourself as a person and as a human being. When we have that, we can feel healthy boundaries and know when we need to say no, or when we need to give in to somebody. We know where our responsibility begins and ends, and where the responsibility of the other person starts. We are often afraid to say no, to show a part of ourselves, because we are ashamed of some of our parts. If we are not happy with ourselves, nobody else is going to be happy with us. This is a very important topic for all of us.

It is important to know the origin of situations where we force ourselves to be something we are not. We often endure other people's behavior, suppressing ourselves, not letting ourselves move forward in life. We are actually not coerced; we don't allow ourselves to be what we are because of fear or prejudice we accepted from society. Through that prejudice we judge ourselves and form an image of what we should be like. If we do not comply with the image of the group consciousness of people in our surroundings, we think there is something wrong with us. That is a problem because it creates an inner conflict that, if it lasts too long, can create disease. We are not being authentic, believing that society doesn't allow us that, while we actually don't give ourselves permission to do that. If other people don't agree with what we are, they don't need to be with us. They can choose a different life path.

There is often a lack of honesty in relationships; it's because we are not being honest with ourselves. Healthy relationships and healthy boundaries are based on self-respect. Such relationships are based on tolerance—we can accept and respect differences in people, opinions, and ideas. Even close people can be different. It doesn't mean you need to accept their ideas and opinions as yours, but you need to let other people be who they are. It is important to know that others have the right to be who they are. It would be boring to live with a person who is exactly the same as us. Often people want to attract a relationship with their twin flame, but this is not a great combination because we are attracted to each other on the basis of our same unresolved issues. Release the need to control others, to have them behave like you think they should. Just like you want to breathe freely within a relationship, it is important to give that same freedom to others.

Embrace trust in the other person—that is very important for a healthy relationship. Trust is built over time, but sometimes it can happen instantly. It is also important to trust the universe. Trust is necessary for building any kind of relationship. We can all have healthy relationships, but first we need to build honest relationships with ourselves. In that way we can both give and receive and have rewarding relationships. The power lies in giving, because the one who gives is powerful; they have the power to give. God has the power of giving and is never weakened by giving—he gives us the sun, clouds, rain, land, life. It is important to give without expectations; therein lies great strength. Through giving we always receive; we do not lose. Everything you have ever given to others remains with you even after this lifetime. Do not calculate how much you have given, and how much the other person has given. Be open to good relationships and the truth. It doesn't mean that you let other people harm you or harass you; through honesty, you will attract people who are honest with you.

5.6 How to improve your relationships

The most important relationship to improve is the one with yourself.

Relationships show us how far we have come in our growth—it is reflected in our reactions to self and others. Our reactions are the measure of our growth. Most of our unresolved issues are in relationships with others. Some spiritual teachers advise us to have relationships—not to be alone—because that will show the result of the many years of self-development. The most challenging relationships are spousal relationships where we live with our partners 24/7. Such relationships show our qualities, weaknesses, and imperfections. The most important relationship to improve is the one with yourself. It is important to accept yourself, be easy on yourself, understand and love yourself. We should be consistent and true to ourselves. If we can accept ourselves, we can accept other people and be accepted by them in turn.

Use the exercises in Chapter 2 to deepen how you accept yourself.

Once we have accepted all good and bad things within ourselves, then we move on to relationships with others. We have already forgiven our mothers and fathers. Now focus on what qualities you need to behave better to yourself and others.

❧ Exercise. Our Relationship with Our Mother and Father

Do this exercise with your mother and father first, and then with other people. Find two or three qualities you believe the other person needs so you could have a better relationship. You will then embrace those qualities in yourself through the Direct Method exercise in Chapter 2. In this way you can heal your relationship with your mother and father, as well as any other relationship that is bothering you.

Ask yourself what this person needs—what virtues, qualities, or traits—in order to be better to themselves, to you, and others. Become aware of those qualities in yourself through the Direct Method exercise; feel them in your DNA, in everything that you are. At the end, do the Gratitude and Grounding exercise in Chapter 2.

This exercise will help improve any relationship. You will feel better in the relationship and your reactions will be better. If you were unsettled by the relationship, you will begin to feel indifferent. The point of this exercise is for you to feel better. Then you will begin to send out different information to people around you, and the way they relate to you will change. Even if their attitude does not change, it is important that it does not bother you anymore. This is the recipe for improving relationships.

❧ Exercise. Our Relationship with Others

This exercise is to enter the space of another person, to see how they felt when they did something, what they were thinking about, what was going on in their life.

We ask to be shown the highest truth about what exactly was happening at that moment, and why it happened. Ask to see what other options could have happened in that relationship. It will then be much easier to forgive and accept that relationship. To forgive, we ask ourselves how we would feel if we completely forgave that person, what virtues we need so we can forgive them, and then we use the Direct Method exercise to look for those feelings and virtues in ourselves. When we find those positive feelings, we feel them in our body. Once we have those feelings of forgiveness, we will see the relationship improve. In this way we can help improve any kind of relationship.

This is not just work on improving relationships, but personal development as well. In this way we grow, because relationships are given to us for growth. We adopt qualities and virtues, become aware that we have them, and find out how we can feel better in that particular relationship, or some other.

The work we do on relationships is work on ourselves. In this way we work through lots of unresolved karma we have come to resolve in this lifetime. Mothers and fathers are the most important people we need to resolve relationships with, then there are our partners and other people in our lives. Once we have resolved that, we can direct our energy to creation, creativity, and other activities that can improve our community and society. Everything starts with us, our mother and father, partner, and other people. Only then can we talk about healing our planet.

5.7 What is our soul family or family of souls?

By working on ourselves, we help the growth of our soul family.

There are people we are deeply connected to and have very close relationships with. We often meet a person and feel a very deep connection to them. We feel they are close to us, like we know them from somewhere; we feel we can confide in them and trust them. We can feel this for our parents, friends, or partners. These are souls that were created together with ours.

Like we have our earthly family, there is a soul family. This is our real family. What is important, is that we share with those people common feelings, beliefs, and a common path. You can have the most trust in those souls. These are the souls you feel will not let you down. This doesn't mean you will not have issues to resolve with them. It is good to know that by working on ourselves, we help our soul family grow. When you resolve something in your life, you help the members of your soul family. Members of your current family do not have to be members of your soul family, but usually at least one family member also belongs to your soul family. We also share our karma and unresolved issues with them. We have the support of our soul family.

There are about 100 members in a soul family, maybe even more. You will often be the leader of your soul family. That means that you influence its development. As we change ourselves, we help them as well. We are a part of the council of twelve. These are the members that hold council and take care of the members of their soul family. When we have the feeling that we are looking after our soul family, taking care of their growth, feel responsible for them, this is the sign that we are a member of the council of twelve, which meets at night and holds council for their family and development of the universe. We travel at night and go to see our soul family. I often joke that we work the night shift; we are always busy.

Your soul family can make you very happy because of this close connection with them, even though you can be physically far away from them. A soul family is very tightly knit; we are very happy when they are happy. You can even perceive the feelings and thoughts of those people when they are not talking. We want to please the members of our soul family; we wish the best for them. This connection of souls is the strongest connection we carry with us. Sometimes our partner is a member of our soul family. In those cases, we have immense trust in that person, but there is no intense sexual attraction or passion in the relationship. Many people live like that, and they are okay with it. It doesn't have to be a problem in the relationship. We change our roles from lifetime to lifetime—sometimes we are the partner, sometimes the father, daughter, or sister.

Many people say that you only live once. It means we need to use our lives well, enjoy the moment and be productive. It is important to be in harmony with yourself, live in the moment and realize your potential. That is why this saying is good, and I agree with it. Still, souls come and go. The soul needs experiences to grow. Earthly experiences give the soul lots of material for growth. The lessons the soul doesn't learn now will have to be learned one way or another. Do not worry whether you will live again; it is a secondary question. It is important to know that people we feel close to are members of our soul family. We meet them all the time, even when we leave this world. They are waiting for us and supporting us.

We can use our soul family to help us manifest something we would like to do. Ask to connect to your soul family. They will appear in front of you. Tell them what you want; ask them to give you their support and blessings, so you can realize your manifestations. Thank them after that. When we have the support of those energies for manifesting our reality, we have a great chance of receiving what we want.

We should be happy that we have our soul family. The earthly family is transient; our soul family always follows us. We were born at the same time, in the same family, and those ties are unbreakable. Be happy for that, and that you have the chance to celebrate existence and life together with them.

5.8 How to forgive others

Forgiving others is the same as forgiving yourself.

We can use all the exercises we used to forgive our mother and father to forgive other people. People do the best they know. Each of us is doing the best we know. We all have our unresolved issues that originate from childhood; there were many things that influenced us and our development. What people are missing is love. They look for it in different ways, in different relationships and activities. Because they did not receive that love in childhood, they project it onto you, searching for the realization of that love. They want other people to make up for what their parents didn't do, although it might not seem so at first. We project our unresolved issues to the outside, looking for a solution outside, instead of within. There is often manipulation and control, leading to conflict.

There are expectations in all relationships. Often these expectations remain unsaid, so the other person is unaware of them. This causes misunderstandings, which lead to conflict, because we have different ideas and perspectives. Suppressing what we want leads to conflict. By forgiving others and forgiving yourself, you allow yourself to grow and move forward. Through forgiveness, you release resentments, guilt, anger, rage, hatred, regret, or remorse. The more we can forgive others, it is a signal we are ready for deeper growth and development.

The person troubling us is teaching us something. They are showing us lessons we haven't yet mastered. Once we master them, we will feel much better in that relationship. For example, the person is not nice; they do not respect you. It is important to see in which part of life you do not respect yourself or others. In which segment of your life do you lack kindness? When you find that out, then you need to adopt this respect and kindness for others using the Direct Method exercise. In that way it will be much easier to forgive others. If we have forgiveness, we will also have love. There is no love without forgiveness. Forgiveness is the biggest manifestation of love. When we can forgive, it means that the love inside of us is great, and it is leading us through life.

We need to forgive ourselves most of all. If we forgive ourselves for everything that we resent in ourselves, it will be much easier to forgive others. We can also forgive ourselves by accepting and understanding ourselves, knowing that we did our best. If we could have done better, we would have done it. Now that we know much better, we will do differently. All those weaknesses are not faults; they are tools for growth, just reminders, the tools we can use to grow and move forward, to become aware of ourselves and expand our consciousness. Forgiveness is a part of the evolution of humanity; we can't move forward without it.

It is important to build respect for yourself, for everything you have achieved, and what you will achieve. This energy of the universe is leading us forward. For the universe to be able to expand, we need to expand our consciousness. We need forgiveness so that our lives can develop, and we can realize our full potential. Without that step we cannot move forward. It is natural; without elementary school you cannot go to college. We would love to skip some steps, but that is impossible. Forgiveness for others is connected to forgiveness for ourselves. We did the best we could; we have the support of the universe, and it is backing us in our efforts. We are troubled by different feelings that cause us lots of problems and take a lot of energy from us. They are the opposite to forgiveness, but we can transform them all if we use methods described in this book. All of those feelings are there to remind us of who we are and bring us closer to God.

5.9   How to find your soul mate or life partner

All relationships that are supposed to be in our lives will happen; they are part of our growth and learning.

This is a topic we are all interested in—many people don't have a partner, and some do, but are not sure whether that is the right person for them. Soul mates are the souls we have spent many lives with, incurring lots of unresolved karma that needs to be resolved now. We made an agreement with our soul mates that we would meet and recognize each other in order to learn the lessons we need to learn. Our soul mates come to us. This is something our souls have agreed upon and it will happen. It can happen for a short time only, although we think it needs to be forever. Soul mates can enter our life briefly to help us learn something. They also benefit from that experience, and then we both move on. It doesn't mean our partnership should be for life. It doesn't mean there is only one soul mate for us. We all have up to twenty soul mates, and it would be good to attract the most compatible soul mate into our life.

There are some prerequisites to attract the right person and have a healthy relationship and life with them—first of all, accepting ourselves as we are. It means we should be happy with our lives, looks, achievements; we should love and accept ourselves, love all parts of our being, even the dark ones, accept them and embrace them. Only then can we expect to be accepted and understood by another person. We need to let ourselves be authentic in relationships and in life, instead of pretending and putting up facades. All of these are essential to attract our soul mate and have a healthy relationship with them. Taking some classes can help us remove blockages that prevent our soul mate from coming into our life. In my Heal Yourself program and Manifesting Love workshop, we work on removing those blockages.

When we think about how we would feel with our soul mate, we do a transformation of feelings. We can ask ourselves what is blocking us from being in relationship with our soul mate, and then do the Transformation of Consciousness exercise. When we feel pleasant feelings, we spread them through the whole body and ground ourselves in that feeling. The less we miss our soul mate, the less we are attached to that idea, the sooner they will come into our life. We can achieve our biggest growth with our soul mates, but they are also the people that can make us experience hell when they trigger difficult things within us. They can bring us to rock bottom, and we can do the same for them. That is why it is so important to nurture that relationship and do our best to make it work.

We should be dedicated to the success of that relationship. Sometimes people don't give of themselves in relationships, or they give only fifty per cent and withhold the rest. They decide not to give themselves fully, and that does not lead to a happy relationship. We should be giving ourselves completely. It is natural to give our whole self to the other person, to have that person inspire and motivate us to move forward with our lives. This is what our soul expects from us. When we give, we grow stronger. Strength and power lie in the giving. Power is in expansion, not contraction to the individual self. Power lies in helping people, not in worrying what is going to happen to us. By giving ourselves in a relationship we do not lose anything. This is how we can achieve a long-term relationship. God is always giving, and it doesn't make him weak. He gives us the land, the sun, water, and heartbeats, and he does not grow weaker because of it.

What you think about yourself is important—like whether you think you deserve your soul mate and love. We should believe we are worthy of that. People are often not able to receive love. The other person can give us lots of love, but we are sometimes unable to receive it, and then we think there is no love. This happens when our back heart chakra is blocked.

Back chakras are in charge of receiving, while front chakras have the role of giving. That is why it is so important to unblock the back heart chakra. It will help our soul mate come into our life, and we will feel that love. We must feel love within so we can share it with others. We expect others to fill us with love, but love is given and shared, not expected from others. Each of us has our own love and we can share it.

Co-dependent relationships are very problematic, when we depend on somebody giving us a drop of love. When we think there is no love in our lives, that we lack love, we will give everything to have it. We developed those holes in childhood, and now we expect other people to fill them. Unfortunately, they have their own holes, caused by the lack of attention they experienced. It is wrong to expect somebody else to fill that for us. This is the reason problems start. We have an idea of what the other person should be like, and how they need to fill the emptiness we have. Actually, we need to fill ourselves with love and share that love with others. Sharing our love with others is a completely different approach to expecting things from them. We all have love inside, because we are made of God's love and each of our cells vibrates in love. We have just projected that love outside of ourselves. We are waiting for somebody to bring us that love, like Santa Claus.

Love will not come to us unless we feel it already circulating in our veins. Then we will be able to share it with others. We will not ask others to be what we want them to be. We will share our lives in love and move forward in life. Then the right soul mate will enter our life. All co-dependent relationships, manipulation, and control need to stop. Only then can a divine relationship between partners come. Then the right person will come and we will be fulfilled.

All relationships before that are on our path of development. This doesn't mean those relationships are bad and we should change our partner. We should grow within a love relationship as long as we can. If there is no more growth, it is time to go our separate ways. If we have created a family and business together but there is no more love and growth, the universe no longer supports such a relationship. That is good, because both sides get an opportunity for growth.

When we are in a relationship it becomes obvious how much we have grown and moved forward. It is easy to tell stories, read books, take classes, and meditate, but you need to show what you have learned in practice. It is easy to convince the mind or ego that we have achieved something in life, have grown and developed, but love needs to be shown in action. Actions are very important. In love and partnership, we show how much we have learned and changed. You don't need to worry about when a soul mate will enter your life. When you are ready, you cannot miss your soul mate. When I think about my own life, I know that I was magnetically attracted to those people. With some people we learn a lot; with some people we go through hell, and each relationship is important and significant. We cannot say that those relationships were wrong; they brought us to where we are now.

Your current relationship also has purpose and meaning; even if you are single, it is meaningful. A relationship with a soul mate comes from your relationship with yourself. What is important is how much we appreciate ourselves, believe we deserve good things in life, how much we have forgiven ourselves, respect ourselves, accept ourselves, and how good we feel in our lives. Only then can we speak about a healthy relationship.

5.10 Who is the right partner for us?

> Trust is most important in a relationship, because without it, there is no growth, development, or intimacy.

Each one of us has a different perspective on the right partner for us, and that is okay. Generally speaking, you should consider whether that is a person who inspires you, encourages your growth, wishes you well, has good intentions, someone you can rely on, who will not let you down, someone you can count on in difficult times, who will be with you, a trustworthy person.

Your partner should be a person who understands you and accepts you as you are, who doesn't want to change you, model you according to their own understanding, or change your life. The prerequisite is that you accept this person as well and show these qualities in the partnership. It is important to accept the person as they are, with all their virtues and flaws, and love them. Trying to impose your own criteria, beliefs, and standards, or control the other person's life, is not healthy for a relationship; it will end sooner or later. Feelings will be suppressed, which results in an unhealthy relationship where someone suffers, unable to be who they are, to express themselves and accept themselves. There is no honesty in such relationships. Honesty is an important foundation for a healthy relationship. It is essential that each person is honest with themselves, showing themselves as they are, not changing for the sake of the other person. Then you can expect the fullness of the relationship and love. A person should have qualities like tolerance, acceptance, forgiveness, and kindness, which are necessary for a healthy relationship.

This is the person that makes you happy when you think about them; they make your day, fill your heart and soul with joy. You are happy when you wake up next to them. Even if they are not next to you, you are happy that they exist. We are all in different stages of growth. In this phase, you are compatible with people who are in a similar growth phase. That doesn't mean that later on you won't be looking for something else. It is important that both partners grow for the relationship to survive. It is not good when only one person grows, while the other stagnates. If both people grow, they will move forward in life. People often have the belief that they must stay with one person for the rest of their lives. That is not necessary. If there is no growth in a love relationship, that relationship is no longer supported by the universe, and it is best for both partners to end it. Partnerships are given to us for growth and development.

You don't need to change partners often to grow. You can grow and move forward in every relationship. Each relationship helps us discover things we are unaware of inside ourselves. In that way we discover our weak spots, where we need to grow and develop. If we have reached a certain phase of growth in a relationship and we cannot move forward, it is important to look for another relationship where we can grow. If you can achieve what you want in your existing relationship, you can find happiness in such a relationship, as long as you are able to express yourself and do not suppress your true self.

An ideal partner is a person who supports you; you know they are by your side even if things don't go so well in life. It is important to be the best version of yourself and let others be the best version of themselves. The highest thing we can achieve in a partnership is unity of existence, where you feel connection to God and the universe through that person, where you feel unity through that person and through yourself. It is complete union; that relationship becomes the peak of existence, or ecstasy. It was intended that we grow and reach that union where you no longer see the difference between yourself and the other person, when we overflow into each other. We all feel the need for that unity of existence deep inside of us.

CHAPTER 6

Spirituality and everyday challenges

6.1 How to reach enlightenment

The universe gives us what we need for spiritual enlightenment.

Enlightenment of the mind and our being is usually considered to be difficult to achieve. We have probably read books and heard stories that enlightenment of the mind or spirit is when we achieve the unity of existence, and we need many years of practice and many lives to achieve it. It is a common opinion that a person must invest and sacrifice many things, give up many things to achieve it. Such thinking is based on dualism, where the idea is that we need to overcome lower parts of our personality to reach a higher personality. It is believed those lower parts must be avoided in some way, or we need to resist them; they should be denied or avoided so we can come to higher awareness. In this way, conflict is created in people and because of that they cannot reach the enlightenment of the mind. They avoid parts of themselves they believe to be undesirable for their growth and development.

We need a different view of reality. The universe envisages everything in a completely different way. It asks us, begs us to be in contact with ourselves, to get to know our purpose here, to live our full potential. The universe is grateful to everyone who helps themselves and others on that path.

The truth is that evolution of humanity leads to the discovery of ourselves to our divine part, becoming aware of ourselves and manifesting our higher purpose. If that is really so, then it would be logical that everything that happens in our lives leads to that. Everything we feel, no matter whether we call it negative or limited, as well as different situations that we label as undesirable, was given to us to lead us to that truth, to spiritual enlightenment. It is not something to be suppressed, denied, or ashamed of. Human nature is such that we have imperfections, flaws, or habits that are not very healthy or acceptable. It can also be thoughts, feelings, and desires that are not acceptable. We should accept that human nature and thank it for being here.

Our lower human nature is not lower at all; it is here for a reason and purpose, leading us within, toward the development of our personality, and enlightenment of spirit and mind. That is what we want. All situations in life are tools for growth, so we should accept them and understand why they are here. They should be transformed into higher consciousness. All those unconscious parts of ourselves will keep creating our reality until we become aware of them and accept them fully. This acceptance is when you say to yourself that you accept everything, when you love yourself and become intimate with the part of yourself you were afraid of, thinking it would destroy your life, and it would be embarrassing if other people found out about it. When you tell that part of yourself to stay with you as long as it wants, that energy is transformed—it is dissolved in love. Energy is transformed and leads us to our inner self.

This part of us has come to teach us something and we can ask it what it is trying to tell us. People fight themselves and judge themselves, analyzing which parts of them are good, and which are not. We resist, don't accept, and live with the idea that things should be different. We have accepted this concept from different books and teachings and then we struggle and suffer. This struggle is endless, and such spiritual enlightenment will take many years and lives. A quick way is to accept your life and see the meaning in everything that is happening to you. Everything has importance and meaning.

If you told a person searching for God or spiritual enlightenment that they already are enlightened, they would take it as a good joke. It would be frivolous, because the person does not see it, does not notice, or accept that. The word enlightenment means to bring light into something—into your mind, into your life. The light is not brought into our life—it is already there, but it is concealed. The sun is shining all the time, you just need to open the curtains so the sunshine can enter the room. In other words, you need to open your eyes to see the sun. We don't see it because it is hidden behind the clouds, because we are in the house or in the woods, but the sun is there all the time.

Your nature is always here; it is not far away. The most natural thing is living in touch with yourself. Enlightenment is the most natural thing we can do for ourselves—accept our light, the beauty of spirit, qualities, and virtues we have within. That brilliance is clouded by our experiences, starting from the fetal period, the first four years of life, then by things we took over from our mother's and father's lives, and beliefs and feelings of group consciousness. The easiest thing is to be in harmony with yourself, to accept yourself. The universe is telling you that you are good just as you are; it accepts you as you are. Recognize why you are like that. Accept it, embrace yourself. Embrace and accept all of your parts, all of your feelings. Accept yourself because you are divine. This is the path to accepting yourself and spiritual enlightenment, instead of fighting yourself. Every feeling we have, everything that happens in our lives is important. It was given to us to recognize, to open the curtains and see the light within. That light will bring us everything we have ever wanted, and much more. We will achieve and manifest much more when we are in touch with ourselves.

People try to make something happen at any price, and by doing that, they block themselves. They have an idea how to achieve something, but they have no contact with reality. That is why manifestations don't work. It was intended for people to have everything they want. This is how humans were created; this is how God intended it and how it should be. Until we stop fighting ourselves, we won't be able to achieve self-realization. We will need many lives to reach enlightenment.

The whole of humanity is heading toward awakening or remembering who we are. We are awakening from sleep and becoming aware of the light we have. I am very happy to be able to offer this knowledge in this way. In this moment, enlightenment is everything you see and feel. Everything that exists is spiritual and divine. Everything is filled with God's spirit and love. God is love—the presence of that love, living and feeling it, putting it into action. Enlightenment is seeing yourself in others, seeing God and yourself in everything that exists. That is the highest expression of love for humanity. Everything we have been running from, all the blockages, anger, and resentment—all of it is here so we can forgive. All those fears are here so we can see how unfounded they are. They are here to take us deeper, so we can get to know deeper parts of ourselves and heal them.

6.2 How to find peace in chaos

Peace is achieved through insight, deep understanding of reality and your life, by knowing why things are happening as they are.

How to find peace in challenging moments and chaos that surrounds us, the chaos of information and disinformation, propagating worries for our future and existence? This is a relevant question, and we have a relevant solution for these problems. There is a way to accept all that unrest, all those fears, and stop running from them. When we accept them completely, they are transformed into higher consciousness, and no longer present a challenge or a problem. We can accept and transform all that unrest, all the worry, anxiety and fear for our lives and our future, everything that bothers us, all dissatisfaction with life, with ourselves, our current situation, and circumstances on Earth.

Use the exercises in Chapter 2 True Acceptance 1 and True Acceptance 2. Try doing these several times until you become peaceful in that area of your life.

Peace is achieved through insight, a deep understanding of reality and your life, by knowing why things happen as they do. We have no control over what happens outside of us, neither in the present nor the past. Knowing that brings you peace, because everything has a purpose and meaning, and everything is transient. Nothing, whatever might be happening, is without purpose and meaning. We can say it is a consequence of the past, a result of cause and effect, but that is not so important; it is important to understand that there is purpose and meaning. We always do our best, just like everybody else around us. Peace comes from accepting yourself and life situations without fighting and conflict with yourself. Peace comes from acceptance of those situations and life circumstances. We accept them and look at how to outgrow and overcome them. We transform them into something that is good for us.

Everything that happens in life is important and significant. The smartest thing is to accept that. The universe allows and accepts everything that happens. All of it was given to us with purpose and meaning. Once we accept that, peace will come. It is important to be at peace with all aspects and parts of yourself, at peace with life, others, the world around you, your family. Faith and trust that everything will be okay will bring you peace. That is faith and trust in the energy of creation or God. Fear and intimidation are methods of dominating and manipulating people. Freedom is living without fear. Freedom is trusting that our lives are already good and will become even better. Everything will come into our lives—love, possessions, and everything we would like to have. Don't let yourself be blocked by other people's beliefs and feelings. Be authentic; be who you are, pure and ready to accept and receive the abundance of the universe—abundance of happiness, wellbeing, and materials. Let us release all fears, worry, and anxiety. We are taken care of.

6.3   How to become free of fear

Fear is usually unnecessary, created in our minds and accepted by others.

Fear is an interesting and relevant occurrence. There has always been fear of disease, of other nations, political leaders, destruction of the world, fear of sin, fear of taking a wrong step, that we are not like we are supposed to be, or what people expect us to be, fear of being authentic, fear of change, of moving forward, fear of life or the future. In my experience, a common fear is existential fear—fear of not having enough, or fear of poverty. That fear has been present in humanity since ancient times, and it is connected to struggle for survival. The key is to learn how to see through that fear, through that illusion we have created ourselves or accepted from others. We don't need to eliminate, destroy, or change the fear. Fear is usually unnecessary, created in our minds and accepted by others—the group consciousness.

At some time in our lives, we have accepted the fear, and we are now living it. For any fear, we can ask ourselves what is the worst thing that could happen. When we see that is not the worst thing and there is no reason for fear, it will go away on its own. It is like when you see something lying on the ground in the dark, and think it is a snake, but when you come closer you see it is a branch and there is no danger. It is the same with fear; when you look deeper into it and come closer, you see there is no reason for it to be there.

Behind all our feelings there is the divine energy of creation. If we knew that all fears stem from the divine energy and cannot appear without that energy, we wouldn't think that those feelings block us or are undesirable. Our feelings carry a message; they are within us for a reason, and when we become aware of the message, they disappear or transform into positive qualities.

The other way is to go directly to the root of the fear and ask ourselves who is the self that is feeling those feelings. When we see our true self, we will welcome the fear; we will see it is completely okay, and we will feel that we are separated from the fear. This will stop the inner conflict, believing we should feel differently and be different from what we are. This inner conflict often bothers us, and it is a huge block for our growth. The key is to remember that we are exactly where we should be, in the right phase of life, developing at the speed that is right for us, with no need to compare ourselves with others.

It is important to completely accept what we are now, because it helps us to see the depth of our being. In that way we see the depth of our existence and grow at our own tempo. Every feeling is important, and so is the fear. Every fear has its message and its significance. It is important to develop friendship and intimacy with each part of ourselves, to feel that all our feelings are okay, no matter what other people might think about that. Our criteria for judging feelings are often prejudice, either absorbed from others or inherited.

Fear is an imaginary creation in our conscious and subconscious mind, without any substantial reality. It can go away as easily as it was created. There are justified fears—fears for our life, in situations when we need to save our own or other people's lives. Those are natural fears, given to us by nature to protect ourselves and react in the proper way. Fear is a natural emotion just like all other emotions, and all emotions were given to us for a reason. They all have their importance and purpose. Artificial fear was created based on beliefs, or other people's fears. That fear can go away when you talk about it with someone, because it becomes clear there is no reason for its existence. A common fear is the fear of public speaking. When you think about what is so bad about public speaking, ask yourself what is the worst that could happen, and you will see there is nothing terrible that could happen. It is the same with the fear of loneliness. We can explain to people they have more time for themselves or can dedicate their time to other things—there are many benefits of being alone. When we are afraid we will not have enough food, it often enough to ask the person when they had a scarcity of food, whether they coped in such difficult moments, such as in a war or other difficult circumstances. We can help people by showing them a different perspective.

Another way of dealing with fear is to feel the fear in some part of the body and ask it what it wants to tell us. Fear is there for a reason. When we ask ourselves what it wants to tell us and receive a positive message, we can become aware of the positive feelings through that answer. We then ask to feel that feeling in the body and anchor in the feeling. When we look at fear in this way, it simply disappears, whether it is a fear of future, of public speaking, or some other fear. The purpose is to find our true being, to realize the divine we have inside of us.

You must have heard that the body is a temple of God, and it has everything we need. Inside the body there is all the grace, all the love, all the riches of the world. There is peace, love, devoutness, greatness, and spirit. That is why the body holds all the answers. Fears come to us so that we can become aware of what we carry inside. The message will be different for each person. For example, one message may be that we should accept the strength we have. Another person will have something else. Once we become aware of that, fears transform into the higher energy we have become aware of. When we realize what message the fear has brought us, it disappears.

We should not run away or hide from fears. They are not obstacles or blocks, but just a roadmap we should follow and see what it wants to tell us. Everything that is happening is good. There is a saying by Sri Sathya Sai Baba that goes: "Why fear when God is here?" What is stronger than God, what is not God's? What is it that can lower our vibration? What is there to worry about if God is here? With this realization, all the fears, all our worries, and anxiety go away. God is here; it is important not to forget that. We are a part of that energy and the more we accept that and become aware of it, all the challenges and problems will disappear and dissipate in the face of that greatness and Divine presence. That presence is within us and around us. When a fish is in the ocean, the ocean is everywhere—around the fish and inside of it. Just like that, we are immersed in God's presence. That is the consciousness of the self, the deepest consciousness around you. There is no place for fear in such a consciousness. Fear has no business there. It can occur—that is natural—it will not persist, but dissolve.

6.4 How to create a better reality and solve financial problems

Everything that will come in the future stems from how we feel today.

People often seek to improve their financial situation, as well as their business and private relationships. We have deep wishes of the soul that arise in us, which are our calling, why we are here, which are part of our purpose. Some of them can be desiring financial abundance, a better relationship with yourself, spiritual or personal growth and development. It is best to write down what you need and what you want. The nature of humankind is such that we always direct our attention at what is missing, or what we see in others, which creates dissatisfaction and suffering. If we had a broader perspective of everything around us, we would be very grateful. The universe is giving us what we can receive at any given moment and guards us from worse things.

Although you may think other people have it much better, that is not important at all; it is important how things are going for you. What we are living now is the best possible option, or reality. It doesn't mean we will not create an even better reality. If we accept this reality and we are grateful for it, then a better reality can manifest for us. It is necessary to be grateful for what happens to us, for the people in our lives, for what we have experienced in the past, and what is happening now, no matter how we feel at this moment. That brings us to new realizations and heals the whole of humanity. It leads us to growth, new relationships, new finances, and everything we want. We don't actually need that new life, because we can be grateful for what we have.

Everything that will come in the future stems from how we feel today. What we have now is a blessing or grace of the universe, of God and laws. Once we can accept that and say thanks for our lives and the money we have, relationships we have, relationship with ourselves and everything we have experienced, then we can manifest a better life. This way of living removes all our money blockages and attracts into our lives everything we need. The focus should not be on what is coming, but on what we have now. We live to fulfill our wishes, and we grow through them.

I am not an advocate of spiritual wishes only, because our souls also need material, tangible things to grow. That is why we need to fulfill those wishes. Know that everything is grace. Accept the joy that comes from gratitude.

The universe is taking care of me, of you, and all of us. Let it take care of your life. Let God take care of the world and you. Although we think we are abandoned, forgotten by God, that has never been the truth. The truth is that everything that happens is grace, and we are immersed in that grace. Try closing your eyes and asking God within you what the highest truth is, why those things are happening in your life. Concentrate on your heart chakra or solar plexus and ask for the truth. When you see that truth, ask God to show you the other options. Then you will see that you are in complete grace, because the other options are much more difficult, with more drama, struggle, and difficulties. That realization will set you free, help you accept your reality, and become grateful to God, the universe, to everybody else, and to yourself. This will help you accept peace and open up for abundance in your life.

6.5 How to realize your wishes and reach your highest potential

Your highest potential is living in harmony with your divine nature.

People often strive for a better job and success in any area. We will realize those wishes if we feel just like we would if they were already fulfilled. Imagine how you would feel if you had that house, partner, money, or possibility to help people develop and grow. Help is always welcome. Maybe you have some projects for your community or town, your country, your family, and friends. Maybe you have a project to improve your health. Imagine having that at this moment, and feel how fulfilled, happy, enthusiastic, joyful you would be, in a deep place of existence, love, peace, presence, and inspiration.

When you become aware of all those feelings, look for them in some part of your body. You may also feel some fears and blockages, but go deeper, feel those pleasant feelings, and ask them to spread into all your cells and organs, so that you feel them as a part of yourself. Thank the universe for that healing, say that you are worthy of it, say that you have the support of your ancestors, soul family, and laws of the universe. Then imagine that you are growing roots into the earth, 100 meters deep down, and 100 meters on all sides. The next step is to ask for support from your soul, your ancestors, higher self, and laws of the universe for success and realization of your wishes. Ask all your ancestors from your mother's and father's sides to come. When they appear, they will be like two great armies in two lines. Ask them to send their blessings and support so that you succeed in what you want to achieve in life, and what you want to resolve. After you have received their blessings, pray for grace to come upon them. Then ask them to go into the light and thank them for their support and blessings. This is the way to manifest anything in your life.

Your highest potential is living in harmony with your divine nature, with your highest consciousness or your soul, when you can be in harmony with the source of knowledge, wisdom, and power. That source sees the solution to every problem. When we are in harmony with the source, we are in harmony with ourselves. When we are able to live with that source, then we are living our highest potential. When we react and make decisions from that level, we then live aligned with the highest potential. Then we do everything we have come here to do, to create, and manifest. That is divine intention, or intention of our soul coming true. We are usually not aware of that, and in this way, we can realize it in our everyday lives.

The point is to live our lives in alignment with our inner principles and values. Realizing your highest potential is a natural thing to do. Living in fear and ignorance is not natural. It is unnatural to look out only for your personal interest, for your own good, not caring what happens to others. Living in fear of the future is also unnatural. It is natural to live your full potential, without any kind of lack in life, whether material or lack of love.

We need to keep coming back to ourselves, finding virtues within ourselves. There are many different meditations that return us to ourselves. In the Integration Technique®, we can find everything that we miss within ourselves. We create feelings within, which then attract those manifestations into our lives. We do this through the Direct Method exercise in Chapter 2, which is a part of this technique. If you have a problem, such as a relationship that is unresolved and troubling you, you can ask yourself: "How would I feel if I had honest relationships, full of love and inspiration?" Maybe you would feel at peace with yourself, fulfilled, or accomplished. Ask to feel those feelings in your body. Discern in which body part you can feel those feelings. Once you feel a feeling in the body, it is important to spread it through the whole body and then ground yourself in the end. This is a simple way to come into contact with your inner being.

All situations and challenges in life are given to you to go deeper into your being and transform the unpleasant feelings. This is the transformation of consciousness happening to you. This is when you feel the dimensions of your soul that were previously unknown to you. It is one of the steps to fulfill your full potential. In this way, the outer blockages created either by us or somebody else disappear. In this way we achieve an easy life, full of understanding, abundance, and love. You can also use this exercise for material, financial, or health issues. Ask how you would feel if things were the opposite of what you are feeling now. Once you accept that as your true nature, watch it integrate into your life. You can ask yourself: "What is my next practical life step now that I feel this way?" This question will connect your brain and mind with your everyday life.

6.6 How to rise again after a fall

> *When joy, happiness, and abundance are just about to arrive, that is the time of greatest darkness.*

Sometimes in life, due to our circumstances, our health, mental state, information we hear from others, or the news, we have a mental downfall—it seems like we don't see the point of existence and this life anymore. This is part of human nature, and it happens to everybody. We should know that things we see and hear are not always the real truth. There is a deeper meaning to why things happen. We are guided, although it is often not in the way we would like to be guided. It is just a developmental phase we go through. These are our downfalls and losses. This is especially the case when we experience loss, when we feel we are about to lose something or have already lost it. All of those situations were given to us for growth and development.

It is important to remain positive, balanced, to talk to someone. That is what friends and therapists are for. In that way we release our heavy thoughts and feelings. The darkness never lasts forever. The sunrise always comes. The most difficult time is just before dawn—that is the time of greatest darkness. When joy, happiness and abundance are just about to arrive, that is the time of greatest darkness. We go through the dark night of the soul; we hit rock bottom. We think we cannot go any further; we see no way out. This is the moment when sunrise is about to come. Stay positive, trusting you will get out of that situation. When we make that change, positive things happen. You need to go out in the fresh air, take a walk, feel the sun on your skin. Nature is like a soothing balm; it loves and supports us. All nature—the sun, wind, water, moon, and fire—they all love us.

We have to accept that love into our lives. Even when we lose the people we love most, we always have God's love. We are surrounded by the love of the universe. You can choose a better picture by saying to yourself: "Let me be happy, let me be better, let me be fulfilled!" Let's be grateful for what we have. You will see, when you say those things to yourself, happiness and joy will enter your life. You can repeat and visualize that. We need to be grateful for what we have. God guides us through difficult life situations so we can get through them unscathed. If it weren't for the love of this universe, we would have it much worse. These are some ways that help us rise after a fall.

Downfalls are normal and we all have them. At one time in my life, I lost all my material possessions. I became a refugee. I didn't have much, so I didn't have much to feel regret about. It is not a nice feeling when you become impoverished, with no house or land of your own. I also lost a loved one; I know what that feels like. I changed many jobs, often starting from the bottom. But now I have created my own healing technique. I see great potential in it to help people and humanity, to raise consciousness, to solve all our past problems that are still bothering us, that are always with us. I see a great opportunity to help people realize their full potential and move forward.

I think that every new beginning is difficult, and it takes time. There is usually a feeling of insecurity, which is normal and follows us through life. It appears when we change our contact with people, our way of working, when we place a new product or service on the market, or want to make a market breakthrough. You want to show people how much it is worth, how good it is. I want to let the divine energy change the consciousness of humanity through me

We should always expect good things. No matter how negative or unfavorable things may seem for us, we should look for a more positive perspective. We should have a vision of all things turning out well for us, visualize everything we expect from our lives, no matter whether we are ill, starting a new business, or we have lost a loved one. Ask yourself what your life would look like if those negative things weren't there, what it would be like if you had the feeling of trust and confidence that everything will turn out alright. Ask yourself what your life would look like then. Invoke the feelings of inspiration, fulfillment, being loved—the feelings you would have if you had a better job, or health. Now find those feelings inside of yourself through the direct method.

Another way is to ask God what other options we could have had instead of the things we have now. Once you see there were other options, much more difficult than what you are living now, you will be grateful for what you are going through. This is the method that will help you accept your current life, to embrace it and say thanks, because it could have been much worse. You could have had a much more difficult disease, much greater problems, much greater losses, or difficult emotional traumas in your life. When you know this, it is easier to accept your life and be thankful.

Gratitude is one of the best ways of raising your vibration. We should be grateful for drinking clean water, breathing clean air, having food we like, for being safe, far away from war. We should be grateful for every moment of our lives. We should be grateful that we were given the opportunity to live now and grow in this time and place. This time on Earth is the most opportune for growth and development. Doing this will raise our vibration and clear all our dark thoughts. It is a good way to help yourself in a crisis, when you experience a fall.

6.7 How to find meaning in life

Each moment is full of meaning, life, energy, purpose, and importance.

We usually have some grand ideas in our heads, and we believe that meaning lies in the realization of those ideas. We think we will find meaning when we realize those ideas, plans, projects, and when we get what we want. When we get the person we want, the job we want, or the finances we want, when we have the car we want, when we get well or achieve something else in life—we believe we will then be happy, have meaning and purpose. We believe everything will be okay, just as it should be. We believe that we do not have any of those things, that there is a scarcity of all that, and we look for meaning in some accomplishment outside of ourselves, in a future that may or may not come. We do not accept this life as it is, as it was given to us. We do not see meaning in it.

Of course, there are people who see meaning in what they are doing right now, in their families, because they have happy and healthy families; they see meaning in their jobs, they are content and happy. I am happy that there are such people, and that they see meaning in everyday things. Meaning lies in those everyday things. From the moment we wake up till the moment we go to sleep there is meaning, just like there is meaning in dreaming. Each moment is full of meaning, life, energy, purpose, and importance. It is full of divinity. That is living in the present moment. That is God's presence, or love. Living in God gives us that meaning.

We get purpose and meaning from living in God, when we see depth in everything that exists, when we see love, joy, truth, when we feel it and live it. The only thing that can give meaning to humanity is surrender to the present moment and God's presence. That presence is independent of what we have, how much we will accomplish, what somebody did to us, independent of the news, inflation, our bank balance, whether we have a partner or not. Each moment is suffused. I call this God's presence, because I know that God is love. We can say it is consciousness, energy of creation, or presence of the highest consciousness.

On my last day in former Yugoslavia, the day before my family and I left as refugees because of the civil war, there was bombing all around our home. I was with my former wife, my sister, and our dog in our flat just reciting the Gayatri mantra for protection. A bomb fell and broke our wall but didn't explode. It went through the wall and into our neighbor's flat. It made a big mess with dust but didn't explode. I believe God's presence and grace saved us that day.

Feeling that energy, seeing it, experiencing it in yourself and others, being with it, working for it and because of it, rejoicing in existence through God, rejoicing in the knowing that God's love is always with us—that means that our lives are fulfilled. You can also call that spiritual enlightenment. It is acceptance of God's presence and life in God. That is the descent of the Holy Spirit on us. It gives us the fullness and purpose of existence, joy, and motivation to carry on, to create, and fill ourselves and our lives with love.

Respect for all creation and for ourselves comes from that, because we are also God's presence. We are an instrument of God. This divine consciousness is within all of creation. It is full of meaning, beauty, and importance. I pray that all of you reading this book live such a life, that God's grace descends on you, becoming a part of your DNA, of everything you are, with the goal of living joy, and creating your lives from that position. Rejoice in every creation and manifestation in your life. Rejoice in the success of other people, because it is your success. Rejoice in every achievement, because it is your achievement. Rejoice in the fact the sun has risen, that it is warm, that all that you have in life was given to you, as well as this possibility of realization and expansion of consciousness.

6.8 How to be grateful

Things are given to us in this universe.

People think they have nothing to be grateful for because they compare themselves to others, looking at other people's lives. They think other people have something better, or something they are lacking. We do not know what is happening with other people. We only see the facade they have created, which is often completely different from their lives and the reality they live. Such comparison is often a cause of insecurity, ingratitude, and unhappiness; it is not productive and cannot help us in life. Ingratitude comes because we often look for what we don't have, thinking that we lack money, luck, or something else. That is not true, because God gives us what we need. Once we realize that, we will be more peaceful and grateful. We have everything that we need in this moment. If we needed something more or better, we would get that. It would be given to us.

Things are given to us in this universe. Good things, and the so-called bad things are given to us so we can learn from them, move forward, and realize ourselves. All those things are blessings, no matter what is happening to us. Every good thing that we have has been given to us as a gift from heaven. The things we call bad, they are also good. We don't see their benefits because we have limited understanding and perception of our lives. Things are given to us, and we should be grateful for everything we have—for the air, water, clothes, our ability to walk, see, and hear.

A few years ago, I was in Thailand. There I caught a tropical ear infection, because I swam in some not-so-pure water. It felt like my ears were full of water, and I couldn't hear anything for two or three days. Only then did I realize what God's grace is, just to have the sense of hearing. I could not wait to go to the doctor to have my ears cleansed, so I could hear again. Just like that, it is a great blessing to be able to see, to touch, to feel, to taste, to be able to walk and talk, to express ourselves. Those are huge blessings we have, and we should be thankful for them. We should be grateful that this body was given to us. We should be happy about it and be content, because the body is a temple of God. We should take care of it just like you take care of a temple or church—you clean it, refurbish it, uphold it.

There are many things we do not see that we can be thankful for. We live like we are sleep walking—in an imaginary reality we created with our minds, and we need to make it come true so we can be thankful. Sooner or later, that will collapse, because it is an artificial structure. When it does, we will ask ourselves where our lives are heading.

I am reminded of a saying by Alexander the Great: "For empty-handed I came into this world and empty-handed, I shall go!" That is why we should ask ourselves why we do something, and whether acquiring material possessions is really so important. We should examine our priorities in life, and why we have lived in the way we have. We cannot take with us even the smallest material possession. It is important to make your life happy in this moment; it is important to think good thoughts, see good in everything. It is important to be proud of your life, be happy that you lived, feel fulfilled. The key is to be grateful to God for every breath, for your beating heart, for all bodily processes. Every second, a miracle unfolds in our bodies. Our very existence is a miracle.

We can stop our egos and the complaining, misery, and feelings of scarcity. Let's finally accept fulfillment, pleasure, happiness, health, love, and creation into our lives. Gratitude raises our vibration and makes us happy. We don't need to wait to get or find something; we should say thanks to God for each moment. Everything is miraculous; our existence, life, and everything deserves respect and gratitude.

6.9 How to make the right decision

All the decisions you have ever made were made according to your best knowledge at the time.

We often find ourselves in situations where we don't know which way to go. When faced with such choices and situations, we use our rational minds to decide. Some of us are too emotional, so we make conclusions and decisions following our emotions. We should include both our common sense and feelings, but intuition can help us the most. It comes from the deeper levels of our being, which surpass the mind. That means we are tapping into a higher consciousness. That is our wisdom body, one of our inner bodies. That part of us should have a leading role when we make important decisions, when we create. Then we use deeper levels of consciousness.

Often people will feel guilty if things did not turn out the way they imagined them. That is not good. Those feelings of guilt, regret, and remorse are unhelpful, and you can work on them. All the decisions you have ever made were made according to your best knowledge at the time. The universe confirms that every decision is a step toward learning, growth of consciousness, and life.

When we make decisions, we are often blocked by the fear of making a mistake or doing something wrong. We do the best we know in the moment, according to our inner structure. We should relax and release those negative feelings. We should act beyond fear. Historically, people who accomplished the most were those who worked regardless of the fear. Such people created, developed, helped themselves, introduced ideas of great importance. They were not led by fear. To make decisions we need courage, determination. We don't need to be fearless, but it is important to be brave enough to stand behind our decisions. We must decide in order to know which direction we are heading in. If you don't have courage and you are overwhelmed by fears, you need to work on them through exercises of transformation.

Once there is no fear, when you embrace courage through the direct method, you will not struggle with making decisions or have inner conflict. Making decisions would not be a problem if there was no fear. We all have inner guidance that leads us in making decisions, we just need to know how to listen and recognize it. We will recognize it as the voice of our conscience guiding us and wishing us the highest good. Once you head in a certain direction, start making decisions, it will be easier. We are often indecisive because we don't know what will happen. We want to control the outcome, but nobody has ever succeeded in doing that. We can always act according to circumstances, our common sense, consciousness, and intuition. We should move forward, rejoice in new days, feel that we are capable and worthy of new things, that we are capable of making valuable decisions. If time shows a decision was not right, do not judge yourself harshly because it definitely had a role in your life. Have the feeling you are worthy, and work on your fears. When you make decisions, it is important to take responsibility for your life and stand by it. Some things can be changed later, but in the moment, this is the way you confirm your decision.

6.10 How to deal with panic attacks

Our true nature is the abundance of spirit.

During my career as a healer, I worked with patients who experienced panic attacks. When a person experiences panic attacks, the body is very exhausted. There is adrenal and kidney fatigue and often there is an overload of toxins, as well as lack of some vitamins and minerals, such as B-vitamins, zinc, and magnesium. Doing breathing exercises is very helpful. You can try the following: breathe in for five seconds, hold your breath for five seconds, breathe out for five seconds, then hold your breath for five seconds before inhaling again. You can also do this by breathing through the mouth. It will help calm down your psyche. Do this at least two to three times a day for ten minutes.

It is also very good to spend time in the sunshine, and swim in the sea. The sea and the sun clean the energy in our auric field. Panic attacks are often caused by the accumulated negative energy we receive from others, especially if we are very intuitive or sensitive. We often collect other people's fears, feel them as our own, and they cause a panic attack.

Oftentimes we have accumulated negative energies in our auras. We cleanse the aura by asking the grace of God to come into our space and clear our aura. You will feel all those negative energies going out of your space.

Panic attacks can be caused by inherent fears. Our fears for survival and existence awaken; people worry if they will have enough money to survive, if their businesses will stay afloat, if they will be able to live normally, and if they will have enough purchasing power because of inflation. Fears and panic become widespread.

Panic is caused by feeling insecure. The opposite of insecurity is not security, but faith, trust, and surrender. That gives us security in God. We all need such faith, just like the trust that we are all guided, that the universe is taking care of us. Other things that can also be helpful are positive thinking, expecting good things in life, trust that panic will also pass just like all the other things in our lives have passed, that new life possibilities will be created, that there will be much more light and love in our lives.

Knowing that there is God or source, life energy, which is full of love, caring, safety, abundance, kindness, contentment, peace, fulfillment, and happiness can help us. We are a part of that energy. That is our true nature; it is what we are—our being. All fears are transient, and everything will pass. We are loving beings, happy by nature, full of happiness, enthusiasm, contentment. We are full of empathy, compassion for others, who wish to enjoy and rejoice, to create. We need to rejoice in our love and be filled with love for no other reason but pure existence. Existence is full of beauty and abundance, tolerance, understanding, acceptance, forgiveness, and enthusiasm for life.

This is where we need to direct our attention and energy. We need to let the panic pass, do breathing exercises, take appropriate supplements supplied by a professional therapist, do Integration Technique® exercises, go into nature, and clear our energies. The key is to always have in mind that our true nature is happiness, contentment, and joy. Our true nature is abundance of spirit, which brings along material abundance. These are transient things in our lives; what we are will remain and last forever. That will heal all panic and fear.

Each time, panic starts with worry. Those feelings of deep worry for you and your future are suppressed deep within you. They are created by unfulfilled wishes and ambitions in us, situations where we didn't find ourselves, didn't feel accomplished, that were left unresolved. After some time, when the situation is favorable, due to outside circumstances or at a certain age, everything that was suppressed will resurface. This can turn into panic if the person does not start creating, realizing their ambitions, changing their lifestyle, their self-perception, and perception of their lives. It would be good to realize that worry and insecurity want to bring us a positive message for our lives, because they are leading us toward a realization of something new. Those are positive moments, although society and doctors will convince you they are not. You may accept this belief and use pills to suppress the worry. In this way we numb the feelings, we do not realize ourselves, nor do we embark on the new path our feelings are guiding us toward. The root of panic attacks is the feeling of not being realized, worry for yourself and your future.

The solution is not to give up, but to take action toward accomplishing what we want, to work and prepare for our goals, start moving in that direction. The key is not to close ourselves off or give up. The easiest thing to do is blame circumstances, life, God, and other people for what happened to us, for being in this situation. We can look at the panic, the circumstances, and our upcoming life in a positive way. This is a positive sign that we have not accomplished something, and we can move forward in that direction. Each action taken in the direction of creativity will contribute to our healing and help us get out of insecurity and panic.

In that way we do what we can; we do our best and handle the situation as best we can. This is how we handle those feelings. We need to take steps in life and remain positive. The time has come to address the fears and finally end that phase, to wrap things up. Everything is positive, and we can move on. We cannot sweep things under the rug, because sooner or later, everything comes out. We are used to suppressing things in life in the name of false security, to keep our relationships, to keep our job, partner, or reputation, to make other people feel good. That can flare up and appear as worry, depression, or a panic attack. Depression is a deep pressure we feel. Panic attacks are one step away from depression, which signals unresolved issues we have been suppressing for a long time. Our system defends in that way; it is slowly giving in and giving up on life. It is good to become aware of all that, because sooner or later it will catch up with us, needing to be resolved.

This is happening to the whole of humanity now—all our suppressed insecurity is rising. It is becoming obvious what we built the security of our lives on—on dubious material things, which can disappear overnight. It is unsafe to build security on outward things, money, work, and other stuff. When difficult situations come, all of it collapses like a house of cards, and then we get panic attacks. To heal completely means to focus on trust and surrender.

❧ *Exercise. How to Transform Fear*

> In this Integration Technique® exercise we locate fears in the body, then ask ourselves how we feel about those fears. We ask what message the fear is conveying, then do the Transformation of Consciousness exercise in Chapter 2. We can put all our fears and accompanying feelings in the bag (True Acceptance 1 exercise) and tell them they are accepted. We can also do the Direct Method exercise in Chapter 2—ask yourself how you would feel without the panic and the fears, then spread the positive feelings through your whole body. Our faith and trust can help us do that.

6.11 How to find lost motivation

No matter how you look at things, life is happening.

Everybody will feel a little discouraged in life sometimes, losing motivation to go on. It can be because of different life circumstances, situations in the world, our private lives, relationships with other people, financial problems, and health issues. Sometimes we have been trying something for years without success; we try to develop some ideas and plans, but things don't go the way we expect them to, so we lose motivation and give up. This is a common occurrence for many people. It would be good to think about how to motivate yourself in such situations. The fact is that life is always moving on. No matter how you look at things or which tune you sing, life is happening. The presence of God is here; creation and creativity are here. Life keeps on moving; we are the ones who give up. We are the ones who have expectations on how things should turn out. People can be motivated to move on and can look forward to life until their very last day. Life is energy and joy, so it can be our motivation. It is important to step out of our programs, patterns, and ideas that life did not give us what we expected, and step into our reality. That is the creative, powerful energy we are often oblivious to, because life is not what we expected.

We often think we are not reciprocated, that we give a lot, but receive nothing, that we are victims of our mothers, fathers, partners, colleagues, clients, friends, or fate. From that position, it is difficult for many people to be motivated to move forward. Life is a fountain that keeps being replenished, filled with clear spring water. Remember how clear spring water is, how full, and when you drink it, you feel it is like a remedy. Life is just like that. Life is beautiful, full of all things new and unforeseen, new possibilities unfolding, realization, creation, and especially love. Love and happiness are what we all search for. We bypass love and happiness because we keep living those movies of lack playing out in our heads. We received that programming from our ancestors, from society, parents, different life circumstances, and it is now limiting us. That was given to us so we could develop, but we were also given a way to get out of those limitations, misery of life, lack, scarcity of spirit, of happiness, money, intelligence, satisfaction, fulfillment, and health.

Gratitude is healing, which is offered to us, which is so simple and easy, but so powerful and good. Gratitude gives you desire, power and inspiration; it gets you into that life flow of love and creation. Gratitude will open your eyes to the beauty that will motivate you to go on, give you the impression that everything is alright. This is not some theory; this is when you see the beauty that surrounds you, when you are grateful for the water, sun, air, the Earth that gives you the possibility to realize yourself here, as a divine and happy being.

Gratitude helps us see that everything we need is here, so we can see that everything that God gives us is here. For example, I love coffee, so I joke that God was in a good mood when he made coffee. Be grateful that all your bodily processes are unfolding, and your body is full of life. Gratitude guides you forward, giving you inspiration and desire to keep on working and creating. Say thank you for your senses, for being able to taste, see, hear, touch all the beautiful things that surround you, for being able to move and think. Say thank you for your divine nature, this uncharted abundance, the unexplored greatness within you. The human body is divinely created and inspired; no car or computer can match our bodies, nor will they ever be able to do so. Thousands of processes go on within us. We were given so many blessings; each moment the universe is giving us abundance and life. Once we become aware of all that, and when we become grateful for each person in our lives, even for our enemies who teach us something, then we will be motivated, have will, power, joy, happiness, enthusiasm, and love. Gratitude is the quality that raises your vibration and guides you deep into consciousness, existence of God, and flow of life.

6.12 How to find your spiritual teacher and energy technique

When a person is ready for a spiritual teacher, they will find them and be led forward in their development.

A spiritual teacher is a person backed by a spiritual tradition, belonging to a certain line of teachers, who came to this planet to help others grow. A spiritual teacher is a selfless person who serves others and can help them in their spiritual growth. Spiritual growth is about developing qualities and traits we have within, which are part of our divine nature, and actively applying them in our lives. The more love we have, the more we love and help ourselves and others, and the more developed and advanced we are. Spiritual growth is the realization of our divine nature in everyday life. If there is no understanding, patience, forgiveness, tolerance, kindness, happiness, peace, or love, we cannot say that we have grown spiritually even if we practice techniques and disciplines. Spiritual teachers come to remind us of the qualities we have within us.

When a person is ready for a spiritual teacher, the teacher will find them and lead them forward in their development. It is the teaching that is important, not the figure of the spiritual teacher. The teacher does what was given to them to do in order to lead others. The knowledge was given through them, they are guided by God or highest consciousness, but the teacher is just an instrument. You are also guided on your path of choosing your spiritual teacher. You will feel that irresistible connection to that person, and the depth of that connection. It stems from many different lifetimes, and the greatest spiritual teacher is God himself, or the highest consciousness, the energy of creation. God guides spiritual teachers and all of us, and takes care of our growth. All techniques are means that help us in our growth, to reach our core and the beauty of our being.

Be careful when choosing your teacher, especially if you cannot recognize that inner connection. Their teaching should have the background of other teachers, of the lineage they belong to. I believe that a spiritual teacher belongs to the teachings that stand behind them and have been there for generations. Be careful who you are surrendering to. You receive energy from a spiritual teacher; you receive an initiation, maybe in an indirect way. A spiritual teacher gives you everything they have, so it is very important who you receive from. With the help of a spiritual teacher, you can achieve the realization of your divine nature. Sometimes you want to be in the physical presence of your teacher, but sometimes that is not possible. It is important to feel the divine energy in yourself and everybody else, not just in the teacher. The goal is to feel the teachings and feel God's presence everywhere.

It is also important to choose an energy or spiritual technique for yourself, because there are so many techniques available. We have a subconscious mind, where all our suppressed feelings are stored, and it creates our reality. Many techniques work on this part. Our lives are created by our souls, higher consciousness, ancestors, soul family, and laws of the universe. We need to take all of that into account. All of those energies and forces in us influence our lives, and according to that, you should choose a modality that you would like to do in order to improve your health, relationships, finances, and love life. The key is to choose what resonates with you.

I was divinely guided, and I believe you can also ask for guidance. I was guided to meet Vianna Stibal and to practice and teach Theta-Healing®, and I brought that modality to Croatia and Serbia. I am also guided by the highest consciousness in my own modality, the Integration Technique®. I was given information I could present to people by creating my own technique. This technique can help people in all areas of their lives. It works on subconscious feelings and different aspects of our being, on inner and subtle bodies, chakras, the ego, soul, all areas of our lives, genetics, group consciousness, soul family, and ancestors, and it is based on feelings.

Feelings are a powerful force that create our reality. The basis of the technique is to feel the feelings in your body, and in this way you become aware of your suppressed feelings. When you are aware of your body, you go out of the mental and open up the path to the inner body, where we use the intelligence of the inner bodies and your physical body for healing. This technique has healed thousands of people including those with physical injuries, respiratory or nervous system challenges, long illnesses, difficult relationships, financial challenges.

There are other techniques, like Reiki, NLP, Access Consciousness, mindfulness, and others. Each technique can help you in life, if you surrender to it. A technique can help you and others. If you want to help other people, you are welcome to all those techniques, because the universe supports expansion of consciousness and awakening of humanity. That is why all those techniques were given to us, because they contribute to awakening humanity and progress.

6.13 How to connect to the present

When you are present with yourself, you are in the present moment.

We have already spoken about connecting with our inner being, but we did not use special breathing exercises to achieve that. There is a tradition of conscious breathing in Buddhism. The basis of this tradition is being conscious of and observing your breath. It is a very powerful exercise that brings you to the present moment. You will notice that I haven't written about the present moment much, because when you are present with yourself, you are in the present moment. When you exit the mind, become aware of your being, you become aware of the presence, being and existence, of dimensions of deepest truth, or consciousness.

You can call this the present moment or deepest consciousness; the name does not matter. It is important to become aware of our part in this consciousness, which is our truth, which is omnipresent, a reality with its own intelligence and awareness.

The following exercise comes from the Vedic tradition, and it reminds us of our reality. It focuses on observing and listening to our breath. When we breathe, we produce the sound called *So Ham* in Hinduism, which means "I am that" (consciousness). That sound is natural, inherent to our breath, it is not a mantra we have added or learned. This is the mantra or sound of our breathing that takes us deep within and connects us with ourselves. It is the meditation for advanced students of spiritual practice, and I would say it is a practice we can all use, regardless of the stage of our development, because it is natural, and it spontaneously takes us into the depth of our being.

❧ Exercise. Connect to Presence, Your Inner Being

> Become aware of your breath, breathing in from the belly, feeling your belly inflate as you breathe in. Breathe in and out slowly. As you breathe in, feel your breath produce the sound *So*, and breathing out, feel the sound, *Ham*. Just observe your breath and feel it. If you cannot feel it, add this sound. Practice this for several minutes, until it becomes your usual practice, and you become aware of the breath the whole time, of this sound that is within us. It is enough to do this for a few minutes a day, when you want to connect with yourself. Observe your breathing and become aware of the sound. You can add to this practice so that you breathe in *So* through your left nostril, closing the right nostril with your thumb. Then use your index finger to close your left nostril and breathe out *Ham* through the right nostril. Repeat this

> several times, while focusing on the tip of your nose. Repeat this until you feel the connection with your own being, or present moment, which is God's presence or consciousness.

6.14 How to release attachments

Things come at the time that is best for us.

It is a part of human nature to be attached to the result of our work. This comes from the need to control. We want to control the outcome of what we do, or what is happening in our lives. That is impossible and it leads us into conflict and suffering. The need to control is the need to have the outcome we want, the result we want. However, that is not really possible, and then we feel frustration. If things are not the way we want them to be, there is disappointment, anger, frustration, and discouragement. We often feel helpless to change our lives or resolve some things. It can be in our love life, business, or finances. We should take responsibility for our lives, which is the opposite of controlling results of our own, or other people's work. We should not attempt to control how somebody will behave or treat us, how others will accept us or see us, how well we will fare in relationships with others or at work. There is a way to get out of this common situation. In the background of everything there is the fear of failure, existential fear, fear of love, and feelings of being unworthy, a lack of self-confidence.

Regardless of the reason for our behavior, it is important to understand that we are responsible for doing the best we can in the situation we are in, and act responsibly to ourselves and others. We should do our best but surrender the result to God's hands. We can say that is surrendering to the universe, letting it take care of things. There is an active intelligence in this world. The universe is conscious—we are the unconscious ones. We operate out of fear and unconscious needs. The universe is aware of us and our actions and takes care of everything. The highest consciousness takes care of the universe, and of us. It doesn't mean you don't have to do anything because someone else is taking care of things. It means you need to do your part and leave the result to the universe.

Let go of the attachment to the results of your work, because that makes us suffer and that suffering becomes unbearable. Life seems to be unfair, as well as other people. We believe we are victims of other people, circumstances, politics, society, state, and others. That is not true. When you are in service of yourself and others, working with good feelings and intentions, and you surrender the result to a higher force, this is called karma yoga in yogic tradition. Even if we do not surrender it to a higher power, the result is not in our hands. Everything happens at the right time. Things that we want will happen at the right time. The dream job will come, as well as the earnings. Everything will come at the right time, because things your soul is yearning for will come true.

Our mind creates unrealistic stories and unnecessary stress, so we compare ourselves to others and criticize our lives; we are angry at the ratio of what we give and receive. Our ego loves drama and tragical stories. Things come at the time that is best for us, when everything is aligned within us, because the universe is waiting for us to align, to become aware of what we carry inside of us, to apply our knowledge, include it in our lives. If we don't let the universe organize things in the way that higher consciousness envisioned it, then we suffer because we do not accept life.

Exercise. Release Your Attachments to Results

> Gratitude is of great importance here. To release attachment to results, or let go of control, it is important to imagine that you are putting all your fears, unresolved issues, and outcomes into a basket. You then carry that basket higher and higher into the sky, until you reach the highest consciousness and intelligence of the universe,

and say: "God, or universe, I am handing this over into your hands, please take care of this." Imagine the basket staying up there, and you come back in peace, trusting that everything will be alright, thinking that you have handed over everything that troubles you, or is unresolved in your life, to the higher consciousness. In the end, thank the universe.

6.15 How to start the practice of conscious eating

Everything we put into our bodies has strong effects on our entire being—emotional, spiritual, and physical.

Many of us are not aware how much the process of ingesting food is important for our lives. Through food we receive energy, strength, and health or disease. What we bring into our bodies constitutes our thoughts, feelings, and building blocks of our cells. Everything we put into our bodies has strong effects on our entire being—emotional, spiritual, and physical. A person can heal through food, if they eat the things they need to get well. The fact is food and water are very polluted today. Our groceries are filled with additives, pesticides, and insecticides. Eating healthy, having healthy habits, being conscious of what we eat and how it affects us is very important for our lives and our total health.

The most helpful foods, with the most beneficial effects on our bodies, are vegetables. Vegetables contain chlorophyl, lots of vitamins and minerals, even protein, and they alkalize our bodies. Many types of food are acidic, and we need a balance between acidic and alkaline. Acidic food includes wheat, meat, and dairy. You want to achieve balance. You are free to decide what you eat, but vegetables are the healthiest foods.

Being conscious means being careful about what you put into your body, and how it affects you. You also need to chew consciously in order to digest food. Saliva in your mouth helps dissolve food, especially complex carbohydrates, so the food doesn't ferment and decay in your bowel. Your saliva will help neutralize toxins and heavy metals from the food. In case of putrefaction, your stool will have an unpleasant smell, and you will experience bloating and flatulence. If the food was poorly digested, your stool will float on water. If digestion was complete, it should sink in water. If you are aware of the process of chewing, you are present, accepting food as God's gift. By being aware and being present you will help the food be digested better.

Before you start eating, you need to give thanks for the food, or say a prayer, asking grace to come to the food and cleanse it, harmonize it with your body so you can absorb it. The food carries the energy of the people who purchased it and prepared it. This is why it is very important to ask for the food to be purified. You never know who handled it, especially if you eat at a restaurant. Even if we prepare our own food, we never know where the groceries have been. Food takes on the energy of all people who handle it, and it influences our energy. The energy of the food is reflected in our bodies. You need to become aware of the process of eating, so you can feel the energy of the food.

We need to be aware that food gives life and energy, and our mood and health depend on it. It is important to take protein, healthy fats, vitamins, and eat fresh and warm food. We should be grateful for the food we receive, grateful to the people who grew or prepared our food, grateful to the universe for having an abundance of food, being able to choose, never going hungry or thirsty. Unfortunately, there are many people on the planet who do not have clean water or enough to eat. We are not aware that it is a gift to be surrounded by so many different foods, by so much love the universe gives us through that food.

It is important to eat fresh food—fruit, salads—and have fresh enzymes for energy. Nuts are healthy; they are full of healthy fats and protein. It is also good to grow your own legume sprouts. I would also recommend drinking the commonly known stinging nettle tea occasionally. It can assist in cleansing blood and the urinary tract as well as assist in maintaining hormonal balance. It is also good to take lemon water, because it contributes to cleansing your blood and organs, removes toxins, and makes the body alkaline. These are my recommendations for conscious eating. Consult your health and wellness professional to ensure these recommendations are suitable for you.

6.16 How to live in peace

All human beings look for happiness, peace, and love.

Everything I have written so far has been with the intent to create peace within. Then we should spread that peace around the planet, abolishing wars, and hatred. Peace should reign in each corner of this planet, and each soul should have inner peace. I would like peace to reign in the entire universe. I do not know what other worlds are like—maybe they are more at peace, maybe not. The work I have offered in this book will contribute to peace coming into your soul and heart, and it will contribute to global peace on the planet, so there is no more imposing, control, manipulation, exploitation, killing for the reasons of interest, vulnerability, protection, defense, or some other reason. I hope with time people will reach a level of consciousness to understand that all those wars, suffering and manipulation lead to nothing.

The only progress for all is respect and appreciation for human life, life on this planet and all that life brings. We should pursue the common good, not just our own narrow interests. That has brought us nowhere and will not bring us happiness and peace, which is what we all want. All human beings look for happiness, peace, and love. These things are inseparable; they are interconnected. If you truly have happiness, you will also have love. If you have peace, you will also have happiness. If you truly have love, you will also have happiness. This is what all humanity wants. We are on the way to making that true in our lives.

Let's take the path of becoming aware of and getting to know ourselves, to develop self-love that is inseparable from love for life and others. If you truly love yourself, you also love others. Those things are not in collision or conflict. By committing to others, you can best commit to yourself and vice versa.

To live in peace, we must be relaxed, because there is no reason for tension. Life plays out on its own, no matter whether we are tense or not. It has played out for hundreds of thousands of years before us, and it will play out after us. It is important to accept life and cultivate gratitude for what we have in life. Laugh, be full of humor—those things go together. Humor and relaxation go hand in hand. You can make jokes at your own expense, not always at others'. Humor allows the higher consciousness to come and open us up for higher realizations, happiness, peace, and love.

When we are relaxed, we have a chance to be in touch with ourselves, our being, and our consciousness. Relaxation is a big key that leads us toward life in peace. This is very much needed in today's world. Things are not serious; they are temporary. Only something that is true can be serious. Everything is temporary and transient. Nothing can be so serious to take away our joy and peace, contentment, relaxation, to make us tense and worry about the outcome.

Give everything over into God's hands, to turn out as it should. Bring a little trust and faith into your lives. I am not asking you to go to a church or a mosque, or worship any particular god, because that is not necessary, but faith and trust in life are very important. Life is eternal and life is true. That is the only serious matter. Everything that comes into life is not so serious. Everything in life comes and goes, and so do we. We are not here forever and for all eternity. At one moment we came, and at one moment we will go away. Just like that, people in your life come and go, jobs come and go. We find our romantic partners at different ages, so partners are also not a serious matter and shouldn't throw you into despair and anxiety. Nothing is that serious. If we understand that, then we understand the transience of this life and we know the steps to peace. It is like coming to visit a new city—you are full of the thrill, and you are not sure whether you will have enough time to experience it all.

Life is just like that; we have come here to stay for a few years, and we need to use them to the fullest, be happy, full of life and enthusiasm. We need to wish for good and beautiful things. Love with your entire heart; fill your glass to the brim—do not let the glass of your life go half-empty. Then peace will come, because it comes with understanding.

You, who are here now, you are eternal. You are indestructible, but this life is a gift, transient, and short. That is why it is important to celebrate life, rejoice in it and be delighted by it.

Let's be the best versions of ourselves; let's not fear the future, let's not regret. Let's accept life! Let's stop fighting! Let's rejoice in what we have! We have a life that we all share on this planet, here and now, and we have enough to look forward to and hope for. We have enough to be grateful for. I would like my book to contribute to trust in life. I will be happy if this book makes a change in a single person; if there are more, I will be even happier. Thank you all who have been helping me, standing by my side. Thank you, universe, for giving me this chance for the truth to be told through me. Thank you, thank you, thank you.

CHAPTER 7

Exercises used in this book

Chapter 2

True Acceptance 1 (page 26)
True Acceptance 2 (page 27)
Transformation of Consciousness (page 28)
Entering Your Heart or Being (page 29)
Intuitive Insight (page 30)
Direct Method (page 30)
Gratitude and Grounding After Your Self-Session (page 31)

Chapter 3

Feelings of Worthiness (page 38)
Healing the Fetal Period (page 49)
Connect to Your Inner Child (page 52)
Make Contact with Your Soul (page 55)
Healing the Separation of the Soul (page 56)
Heal the Evolutionary Path of the Soul (page 57)
Descending of the Soul into the Body (page 59)

Chapter 4

Know Your True Being (page 69)

Chapter 5

Receive Love: Unblock Your Back Chakra (page 82)
Feel Universal Love (page 84)
Our Relationship with Our Mother and Father (page 90)
Our Relationship with Others (page 90)

Chapter 6

How to Transform Fear (page 125)
Connect to Presence, Your Inner Being (page 130)
Release Your Attachments to Results (page 132)

CHAPTER 8

Integration Technique® Heal Yourself training program

Interested in learning more about Goran Karna's transformational training programs?

Become an Integration Technique® practitioner through structured, experiential, and deep training.

The Integration Technique® Heal Yourself program comprises four levels of training, plus an Advanced Healing workshop. The program leads you on a healing journey by connecting you to the wisdom of your body, and your innate capacity to recognize, accept, transform, and heal yourself and your surroundings.

WHAT WILL YOU LEARN IN THE HEAL YOURSELF LEVEL 1 TRAINING PROGRAM?

- How to use your body's intelligence to transform your feelings, thoughts, beliefs, and everything that blocks you in your life
- How to awaken your intuitive senses and develop intuition
- How to work on physical disorders
- What Koshas or inner energy layers are, and how they affect your life
- How to heal traumas from the pre-fetal period, the fetal period, and the first six years of your life

- How to manifest your reality
- How to connect with your Being or Energy of creation within you
- How to heal your ancestors and soul family
- And much more …

WHAT WILL YOU LEARN IN THE HEAL YOURSELF LEVEL 2 TRAINING PROGRAM?

- How to transform and balance your ego
- How to heal the feeling of separation, common to all humanity
- How to free yourself from karma and karmic patterns
- How to heal the traumas of the soul and the developmental path of the soul
- How to work on the subtle bodies and heal them—etheric, mental, emotional, and astral
- How to heal all seven chakras, including two additional chakras—the Earth Star and Hara
- How to overcome limitations of collective consciousness
- How to expand your own consciousness

WHAT WILL YOU LEARN IN THE HEAL YOURSELF LEVEL 3 TRAINING PROGRAM?

- How to work on the physical body, organs, and miasmas (genetic predispositions for certain illnesses, emotional states, and patterns of behavior)
- How to heal the higher chakras and subtle bodies
- How to forgive your mother and father
- How to work on self-love and love for your physical body
- How to accept and heal your wounds
- How to free yourself from suffering
- How to work on the virtues of trust and surrender

WHAT WILL YOU LEARN IN THE HEAL YOURSELF LEVEL 4 TRAINING PROGRAM?

- How to work with DNA patterns and cellular memory to release ancestral burdens
- How to heal trauma and liberate your system from the impact of abuse
- How to explore past lives and their influence on your current life experience
- How to face and transform fear at its root
- How to work on addictions and unhealthy energetic connections
- How to release patterns of self-centeredness and over-identification with the ego
- How to awaken and refine your intuition and inner knowing
- How to support the brain and nervous system through conscious bodywork
- How to activate your body's natural power for regeneration and rejuvenation
- How to open yourself to your higher purpose, soul guidance, and inner truth
- How to move toward self-realization and the embodiment of your true essence

ADVANCED HEALING WORKSHOP

This workshop takes you on a journey of self-healing and empowerment, enabling you to deepen your impact on others.

When we bring awareness and understanding to our unconscious or subconscious, we open the door to healing. This process helps us expand our awareness and illuminate those tucked-away feelings, traumas, and recurring patterns in our lives, paving the way for their healing.

In the Advanced Healing workshop, we dive into advanced healing techniques and seamlessly integrate them with your existing skills. Our emphasis on heightened awareness and intuition training will empower you to achieve faster, more effective, and deeper healings.

WHY FOCUS ON INTUITION?

When you discover the significance of intuition in healing, you unlock the following benefits:

- Personalized Healing—enables you to create a tailored approach that aligns with the specific needs of each individual.
- Holistic Understanding—provides deeper insight into the interconnected aspects of physical, emotional, and spiritual well-being.
- Uncovering Root Causes—enables you to explore the root causes of issues for a more comprehensive healing process.
- Facilitating Transformation—allows you to introduce innovative and transformative approaches to healing.

Workshop Highlights include:
- New advanced healing techniques
- Focus on awareness and intuition
- Live demonstrations by Goran, followed by hands-on practice
- Reduced therapy sessions for complete healing

About the author

Goran Karna is the founder of Integration Technique®. He was born in Croatia. He graduated with majors in philosophy and art history at the Faculty of Philosophy in Zadar. In Australia, he received a Diploma in Natural Therapies—Homeopathy at Health Schools of Australia. He is also certified in Yumeiho massage and has studied vibrational healing in India. Goran received a Certificate in the Science of ThetaHealing® at the Theta Healing Institute of Knowledge (THInK®), Idaho Falls, USA.

From the earliest age, Goran has been interested in spirituality and studied different religions, spiritual movements, and meditation. His spiritual teacher, Sri Sathya Sai Baba, has influenced his life and work significantly. In Australia he came to know Vianna Stibal and the ThetaHealing® technique. After that, he brought this technique to Croatia and Serbia.

He has held over 500 different classes and workshops. In his healing practice, he has been successful in treating physical illnesses, emotional problems, traumas, fears, relationship problems, and financial problems. Through his many years of working with people, Goran has seen the ways and methods that can most easily bring people to deep healing, that help people move forward in their lives and make the next step. From his great love for people and contribution to the world came this modality, the Integration Technique®. Its message is true acceptance of ourselves and living life in harmony with our own being.

In March 2020, due to a Staphylococcus infection and coronavirus, he had a near death experience in Finland and lay in an induced coma for ten days. After that, he began developing this technique. He developed the Heal Yourself training program in four levels and teaches online workshops and webinars.

For more information, visit: www.gorankarna.com
Email: goran.integration@gmail.com

www.ingramcontent.com/pod-product-compliance
Lightning Source LLC
Chambersburg PA
CBHW072005290426
44109CB00018B/2141